ODD DESTINY

☆   ☆   ☆

MILTON LOMASK

This Slender Reed
A Life of James K. Polk

John Quincy Adams
Son of the American Revolution

Andy Johnson
The Tailor Who Became President

"I Do Solemnly Swear . . ."
The Story of the Presidential Inauguration

ODD DESTINY

A Life of Alexander Hamilton

☆ ☆ ☆ ☆

by Milton Lomask

Farrar, Straus & Giroux / New York

92
Ham

Since one of the nobler beings, second only to

guardian angels and honest mechanics,

is a good reference librarian,

this book is for Mrs. Eileen Donahue of

the Library of Congress.

Contents

1   Island Boyhood   *3*

2   The Fuse of War   *15*

3   With Pen and Sword   *28*

4   The Little Lion   *45*

5   Love, Economics, and Glory   *64*

6   Nation-Builder   *79*

7   Supernatural Thunders   *102*

8   Fox Hunt   *122*

9   "Mine is an odd destiny"   *134*

10   Interview in Weehawken   *161*

Bibliography   *173*

Index   *177*

"Mine is an odd destiny . . ."

Alexander Hamilton

ODD DESTINY

☆   ☆   ☆

1

Island Boyhood

"There are strong minds," Alexander Hamilton noted in the third decade of his life, "that will rise superior to the disadvantages of situation, and command the tribute due to their merit." These words appeared in a political pamphlet, but obviously Hamilton was thinking of his own rise to fame after a discouraging boyhood on the little islands of Nevis and St. Croix in the West Indies.

Although his parents, James Hamilton and Rachel Fawcett Lavien, lived together for fifteen years, they were never married. Daughter of a Nevis physician of French descent, Rachel grew up in the shadows of a broken home. Shortly after her birth in 1729, her parents separated, and Rachel seems to have spent the remaining years of her childhood with the mother. At sixteen she became the wife of John

Michael Lavien, a German-Jewish merchant and planter living on St. Croix. Gertrude Atherton's vivid biographical novel, *The Conqueror*, pictures Rachel's mother as forcing her beautiful and spirited daughter into a loveless marriage with a wealthy man. Actually Lavien was not wealthy, although the older woman may have thought he was. Perhaps because of recurrent financial crises, perhaps because Lavien was at least ten years older than his wife, their union was a stormy one. Rachel had left her husband and had returned to her now widowed mother when in the early 1750's James Hamilton came to the West Indies.

Came with a flourish, for he was that sort of man: elegant, dapper, ingratiating, and unstable. Tall and darkly handsome, he was the fourth-oldest of the nine sons of Alexander Hamilton, Laird of Cambuskieth or Grange in southwest Scotland. Like Lavien, he was considerably older than Rachel, but this did not prevent their falling in love. Nor did Rachel's marriage deter them from living under what their tolerant West Indian neighbors regarded as a respectable common-law arrangement.

From her father Rachel had inherited a large stone house on the outskirts of Charlestown, chief city of Nevis. Here she and James Hamilton established their home; and here their sons were born, first James in 1753, and then Alexander, whose date of birth is in dispute, although good evidence would make it January 11, 1755.

Then as now, his island birthplace was a British possession. Only eight miles from north to south and only six miles across, Nevis rests on the blue-green waters of the Caribbean like a wagon wheel with a very high hub. The hub is Mount Nevis, an extinct volcano, 3,596 feet above sea level. A white cloud wraps the mountain's cratered summit. Vir-

gin forests darken its shoulders. Athwart the slop
spiral the carefully tended fields and coconut groves of
big plantations. Still farther down lie the island's landing
sites, with Charlestown, the largest of them, overlooking the
tossing breakers of the narrow strait between Nevis and the
somewhat larger island of St. Kitts to the west.

The caress of the trade winds during the long and balmy
winter, the flash of tropical birds across sunlit skies, the fruit
trees bright with blossoms in the spring and thick-hung with
guavas and bananas in the early fall, the many-colored
blooms of lush shrubs and swelling vines—these, and the
stunning views of the sea from every hill, make the island of
Nevis as close to a paradise as any speck of land on earth. A
quiet little corner of the Caribbean today, it was a carnival
of activity in Alexander's time. In the eighteenth century
the whole world hungered for the products of the West Indian sugar cane. On Nevis every tillable acre went to its cul-
tivation. In the autumn planting season an army of slaves
marched across the land, digging holes to receive the tender
sprouts. At "crop time," fifteen months later, they marched
again, cutting the ripened reeds and bearing them away to
grinding mill and boiling house. In the harbor of Charlestown, ships flying the banners of a dozen nations waited at
the long, tall jetty, their owners eager to exchange American
lumber and English woolens for West Indian sugar, molasses, and rum.

The capital city had less than two thousand inhabitants,
but its echoing arcades and busy waterfront yielded the ever
changing sights and sounds that stir the blood and awaken
the mind of a growing boy. The products of the sugar cane
were not its only wealth. Charlestown was the slave market
for much of the Caribbean. Rarely a month passed without

ainey" ship from Africa, its airless
with men, women, and children.
sters went up throughout the islands,
obable date of the ship's arrival, the
cargo, the hour of the auction in the three-
re. As soon as the vessel nuzzled the Charles-
endants in the employ of the slave master
egroes onto the dock, washed them with salt
wa aved them with oil. Then, with a small boy stepping ou smartly in front and hammering a drum, they
marched them to the square to be sold to planters and merchants from all over the Indies. It is a certainty that Alexander witnessed some of these spectacles. Inevitably they hewed
to his memory. Years later, his hatred of human bondage
would take the form of a long and effective leadership in the
struggle to abolish slavery in the state of New York.

His father had come to the West Indies in search of a fortune and never found it. For a time he held a partnership in
a prospering commercial firm. When Alexander was born,
however, this position had already gone. James Hamilton
was working when and where he could, usually as an agent
for one of the local merchants. In 1765 a job of this sort took
him to St. Croix, then a part of the Danish West Indies, now
the largest of the American-owned Virgin Islands. Rachel
and the boys accompanied him, and a house was rented in
Christiansted, main seaport and capital of the island. James
Hamilton did not linger there long. Within a year another
business errand took him to a different island. Neither Alexander nor his mother ever saw him again.

If Alexander resented his father's desertion, he hid his
feelings. The two of them corresponded at frequent inter-
vals. Years later, after the son had become famous, although

never rich, he often saved the older man from want by sending him sums of money; these eventually totaled thousands of dollars. During his adult life, Alexander seldom mentioned his mother, yet she stood by him as long as she lived. His charming scamp of a father he mentioned often, and always with respect. One of Hamilton's biographers, John C. Miller, has offered a convincing explanation for this curious behavior. Sensitive to the point of belligerence about his illegitimate birth, Alexander Hamilton was fond of reminding people that the "best blood of the British empire" flowed in his veins. He never forgot that he owed that "blood" to his father, the son of a lord; that his descent from a noble Scottish house was his ticket to the homes and society of the American rich.

James Hamilton's departure from the family circle in 1766 left Alexander's mother with two small sons to support. It is a clue to her character that she proved a better provider than their father had been. She opened a store in her home, selling salt pork, butter, and flour to the island planters. She found jobs for the boys. James she apprenticed to a carpenter. As for Alexander, when a sudden fever ended his mother's life on February 18, 1768, he was totting up sums and examining bills of lading for Nicholas Cruger, owner of Beckman and Cruger, an import-export firm with a store and warehouse in downtown Christiansted, one or more trading vessels riding at anchor in the nearby harbor, and intimate ties with Kortright and Cruger, one of the older mercantile establishments of New York City.

Nicholas Cruger belonged to a family that had given New York two mayors and a founder and first president of its powerful Chamber of Commerce. Nicholas himself had engaging qualities—courage, honesty, cordiality, and perception enough to realize that in Rachel Lavien's small and fine-boned son, with his reddish-brown hair and almost pretty face, he had an exceptional employee. Young Hamilton minded neither hard work nor long hours, and when he was not leaning over his high bookkeeper's desk, he stocked and sharpened his mind by reading good books and writing bad poetry. Under Cruger's friendly guidance, he advanced rapidly. By 1771 he was the firm's chief clerk. When, in November of that year, ill health took Cruger to America, he left Alexander in charge of his business.

Much has been made of the aplomb with which for five months the sixteen-year-old clerk filled his boss's shoes. Too much perhaps. In the brash, growing, hard-working, and hard-living New World of the eighteenth century there was no such thing as a "teenager." At age fourteen or fifteen, a boy put his childhood behind him to shoulder the duties of a man. This is not to suggest that Alexander's managerial performance was unsatisfactory. His skill in coping with Cruger's customers—rough ship captains and shrewd traders—points to a swiftly maturing understanding of human nature. His handling of the firm's accounts and correspondence speaks well for his previous schooling.

Just what that schooling consisted of is unknown. He himself once spoke of having studied briefly with a Jewish woman when he was still so small that she stood him on a table for better visibility when it came his turn to recite the Ten Commandments in Hebrew. Presumably the rest of his early training came from his mother and, after her death, from the relatives or friends who took him in. At sixteen he was writing precisely in French, was adept at simple mathematics, knew something about the physical sciences, and was familiar with the writings of Plutarch, Pope, and other classical authors.

His work for Cruger added a rich dimension to his education. Cruger's customers came from all points of the compass. With them came the flavor and sparkle of distant hives of human enterprise such as London and New York, Copenhagen and Philadelphia. On Christiansted's noisy wharves, Alexander learned at an early age that men are not angels. Greed and selfishness, he discovered, often rule a man's actions—a lesson that in time would help shape his personal political philosophy.

Unhappily, the experiences that broadened and brightened him also made him discontent. The more he heard of the great world outside, the deeper grew his longing to be a part of it. In 1769 his friend, Edward Stevens, left St. Croix to become a student at King's College, now Columbia University, in New York City. Alexander remained in Cruger's counting house, but his mind dogged Edward across the waves. Not mighty England but England's thriving colonies in North America were the natural lodestone to a young man whose warmhearted employer was an American colonial by birth and whose best friend was now writing him of the stimulating bustle of fast-growing Manhattan.

To Edward, a youth of his own age, Alexander could reveal the troubled thoughts behind the polite and smiling exterior of the mercantile clerk. Except for his job, there was little to interest him in the West Indies. His maternal grandmother had died years before. Since Rachel's death, he and his brother James had drifted apart. They had never had much in common. A simple, plodding fellow, James would live out his days in the islands, seemingly content with the little these picturesque but remote outposts of civilization could offer. Of his mother's surviving relatives in the area, Alexander was on consistently intimate terms with only one, Mrs. Ann Lytton Venton, a cousin twelve years his senior.

Later, after a second marriage to a man named Mitchell, Ann would move to America where Alexander would be of some financial assistance to her.

What then, he asked his friend in New York, had he to look forward to in Christiansted, population four thousand? In time no doubt Nicholas Cruger would offer him a junior partnership. After that he, like Cruger, might marry a daughter of one of the old island families and end up living in one of the palatial stone mansions that lorded it over the sweeping cane fields of St. Croix. For so proper and comfortable a vision as this there was no room in young Hamilton's highly colored dreams. "[T]o confess my weakness, Ned," he wrote his friend, "my ambition is prevalent, so that I contemn the grovelling condition of a clerk or the like . . . and would willingly risk my life, though not my character, to exalt my station. I wish there was a war."

I wish there was a war! It is startling how that simple statement in the earliest of Alexander Hamilton's surviving letters flings open the door to his character. Human combat in all its forms: war and glory, conflict and argument, challenge and danger—as long as he lived, his audacious nature would crave those things as ardently as a scholar yearns for quiet or a gambling man for attractive odds.

It was not a war, however, that was to release him from his island prison; it was a good friend and a violent storm.

The friend was the Reverend Dr. Hugh Knox, a handsome Presbyterian minister and self-trained physician. Scottish by blood, Knox appears to have begun life in Ireland. In 1751, in his eighteenth year, he emigrated to America, taught school briefly, sowed a few wild oats in the village taverns of Delaware, and then enrolled in the College of New Jersey, now Princeton University, where after earning his degree he studied theology for a year under the college's genial president, the Reverend Aaron Burr, father of the more famous Aaron Burr whose life was to be so dramatically entwined with Alexander Hamilton's.

In 1755 Knox sailed for the West Indies to become pastor of a church on the island of Saba, a day's boat ride from St. Croix. Even smaller than Nevis, Saba is little more than a scarred and tapering mountain rising from the sea. For seventeen years Knox tramped its jungle paths and mountain lanes, instructing the plantation hands in the stern doctrines of Calvinism and tending to their medical needs. The year 1768 saw the publication of some of his sermons. These bring to view a brilliant preacher with a genuine literary gift.

In the spring of 1772 he transferred to a larger church in Christiansted. He and young Hamilton might have met earlier, as Knox had spent time on St. Croix during the preceding year. No matter when their association began, it ripened rapidly into friendship, the older man making a lasting impression on the younger one. A sometimes muted but unmistakable religious strain runs through much of Hamilton's writing. Childhood training accounts for its origins, but his intimacy with Knox enormously deepened and strengthened it.

Knox saw Alexander's problem with the sympathetic eyes of experience. His years on tiny Saba had shown the minister-doctor how frustrating life can be for a gifted man chained to an area devoid of outlets for his abilities. Looking at Alexander, he saw the flower in the bud. Since he was a perceptive man, he probably also spotted the weakness there, that craving for danger as an opportunity to prove himself that would sometimes carry Hamilton too far and one day kill him. To the kind-hearted cleric one point was abundantly clear: the younger man's talents must not be allowed to go unused. He must be sent to America as soon as possible; he must complete his education in one of the mainland colleges. But ocean voyages and college educations cost money. A poor man, Knox could only say his prayers and hope that Providence would point the way.

The "way" opened soon and dramatically. On St. Croix, as throughout the Caribbean, the winter weather is a delight —cool mornings and cool nights, with the trade winds putting a pleasant edge on the noonday heat. With the opening of the hurricane season in early summer, a disturbing change occurs. During this period the trade winds often turn murky. Sometimes, as the West Indians say, they "go into hibernation," blanketing the region with a hot, suffocating stillness. With every shift of the wind, heads rise, eyes searching the distant horizon for the dirty rim of black cloud that presages disaster. First-degree hurricanes are rare, averaging only about one a century, but the fear that this season may bring that one infects the atmosphere like a fever. To bolster their spirits, the people give voice to a jingle. "In July, watch sky," they chant. "In August, watch dust. In September, remember. In October, thank God, 'tis over."

On the last day of August, 1772, one of the worst hurricanes in West Indian history struck St. Croix at dusk. For six hours the shrieking, clawing winds did their work.

When it was over, Alexander described what he had witnessed in a letter to his father. "The roaring of the sea and wind—," he wrote, "fiery meteors flying about in the air— the prodigious glare of almost perpetual lightning . . . were sufficient to strike astonishment into Angels. A great part of the buildings throughout the Island are levelled to the ground . . . whole families running about the streets unknowing where to find a place of shelter—the sick exposed to the keenness of water and air—without a bed to lie upon—or a dry covering to their bodies—our harbor is entirely bare." In all this the young author saw the hand of God. His minister-friend had taught him well. "Where now, Oh! vile worm," he demanded of mankind in general, "is all thy boasted fortitude and resolution? What is become of thy arrogance and self-sufficiency? . . . See thy wretched helpless state and learn to know thyself. Learn to know thy best support. Despise thyself and adore thy God."

Before sending these words to his father, Alexander showed them to Knox. The delighted minister made a copy of the letter and sent it to a local newspaper. If Knox's purpose in publishing the letter was to enlist support for Alexander's hopes, he had reason to congratulate himself. Influential men on St. Croix and the other islands pronounced the letter a remarkable piece of writing in view of its author's youth. Some went further. They dug into their pockets and subscribed to a fund that would enable the young author to leave the Caribbean. Sweet charity was not their only motive. The island lacked doctors. Some of them assumed that, like his friend Ned Stevens, Alexander would study medicine in America and then return to his homeland. Later he did consider a medical career, only to be drawn into other fields by the clamorous events of a country rushing into war.

The most generous of his patrons was Nicholas Cruger, his boss. Cruger disliked losing his best employee, but he was a big enough man to accept Knox's argument that the talented clerk should have his chance. Boston was the destination of the ship that in October of 1772 bore the young man away from the West Indies forever. Within a few weeks, however, another ship would carry from St. Croix a quantity of sugar, molasses, and rum consigned to Kortright and Cruger of New York City and accompanied by a letter from Nicholas Cruger authorizing his American associates to apply the proceeds from these items to the support and education of Alexander Hamilton.

2

The Fuse of War

The America of 1772 was an ideal place for a young man burning to take part in the larger events of his times. Alexander Hamilton's ship, the *Thunderbolt*, docked at Boston. The little town on its hilly peninsula was only a stopover on a journey that the Reverend Dr. Knox appears to have planned for his protégé in considerable detail; but whether Alexander tarried there a few days or a few hours he could scarcely fail to sense the tensions in the salty air.

For nearly a decade New England's major seaport had been the storm center of the increasingly corrosive dispute between the American colonies and the rulers of Mother England across the sea. Of the issues involved, the seventeen-year-old from the West Indies could hardly have been unaware. Both of the men chiefly responsible for his journey,

Knox and Cruger, had for years been outspoken supporters
of the American cause.

It was one thing, however, to have heard about the great
quarrel at second hand. It was another to be in the thick of
it, to listen to the arguments echoing in every Boston inn
and tavern, to read the flaming words of rebels, writing in
the local press over such pen names as "Humanity" and
"Oliver Cromwell." Humanity insisted that, in view of England's unfair colonial policies, "Americans would be justified in the sight of Heaven and all nations . . . in forming
an independent government of their own." Oliver Cromwell declared:

> *Our wives & our Babes, still protected shall know*
> *Those who dare to be free shall ever be so;*
> *On these Arms & these Arts they may safely rely,*
> *For as* FREEMEN *we'll live, or like* HEROES *we'll die.*

Two years had elapsed since the winter evening when in
Boston's King Street a squad of British redcoats had fired
into a mob of taunting citizens, killing five; but in such popular gathering places as the Bunch of Grapes in State Street
or the Three Doves in Marlborough Street, indignant patriots still talked of the "horrid massacre." The thirteenth
anniversary of George III's accession to the throne, falling
on October 25, shortly after Alexander's arrival in the
city, engendered the usual military exercises on the Common; but for every volley fired in honor of His Majesty, a
hundred curses rained on His Majesty's Parliament and
ministers for daring to regulate American commerce and tax
American citizens without their leave.

Since the only attempt so far to establish a stagecoach line between Boston and New York had failed, the traveler had to make the next lap of his journey by packet, sailing southwest along the New England coast, then northward past Sandy Hook and through the Narrows. Thus he first saw New York as countless immigrants after him would see it—from the waters of its broad bay.

The eighteenth-century city occupied only the foot of the big island it would later vastly outgrow, but to Alexander, accustomed to the small trading centers of the Caribbean, it must have looked unbelievably large and tremulously alive. No one yet had bothered to compile its vital statistics, but an informed estimate put the population at twenty-eight thousand. It had a hospital, a college, two prisons, several miles of paved roads and stone sidewalks, and thirty-four hundred houses, most of them finished in the precisely pointed red brick favored by the original Dutch settlers. Visiting Europeans, familiar with the seaports of the Old World, marveled at the number, the busyness, and the size of its docks, some of them reaching so far into the city's watery boundaries—the East and Hudson rivers—that their front pilings rested in forty feet of water.

At the southwest corner of the island, where the two rivers joined to form the bay, spread a tree-shaped parade ground known as the Battery, with the glowering walls of Fort George rising from its high hill. In front of nearby Government House lay the small oval park called Bowling Green. Extending northward from the green, Broadway, the principal thoroughfare, divided the city into unequal halves, with much the larger section to the east. Landmarks along Broadway were Trinity Church at the head of Wall Street and St. Paul's Church across from "the fields," the park or common where New York's city hall now stands. As far up as

Chambers Street the city was thickly settled, from there to Houston Street only sparsely so. Above Houston was largely primeval forest, broken by farms or country estates and by the little settlements of Greenwich, Chelsea, Murray Hill, Bloomingdale, and Harlem.

Like Boston, the New World's second largest city was only a stopover for Alexander. In New York, however, he had much to do. He called at Kortright and Cruger to review his plans with his advisers there. An education was the purpose of his trip, and the decision of his friends at the big mercantile firm was that he should prepare himself for an American college by studying for a period at the academy run by the Presbyterians in Elizabethtown, capital of the province of New Jersey. From Kortright and Cruger he branched out to other parts of the city. The Reverend Dr. Knox had given him letters of introduction to a number of local ministers. One of these took him to the study of the Reverend Dr. John Rodgers, formerly of back-country Delaware, now pastor of two of Manhattan's twenty churches. Years before, Rodgers had helped Hugh Knox get a start in life even as Knox was now helping Alexander. Perhaps the New York cleric amused the visitor with a story about their West Indian friend: how one Saturday afternoon during his carefree youth, Knox regaled the customers of a rural tavern by delivering a mock sermon in the oracular manner of the Reverend Dr. Rodgers himself, an imitation so accurate that instead of laughing at what was intended as entertainment, Knox's drunken listeners fell to weeping over their sins and hoarsely resolving to lead better lives.

The stranger was not left to find his way about on his own. Kortright and Cruger furnished him with a guide, a step that turned out to be the highlight of Alexander's first visit to the city that would someday be the center of his world. His guide was Hercules Mulligan, owner of a men's shop specializing in "superfine cloths of the most fashionable color" and brother of a Kortright and Cruger executive. Physically, the thirty-two-year-old merchant conformed to his first name—a large, muscular man, forceful and direct. If Alexander was not already a "warm Whig," a patriot, he very likely was well on his way to becoming one after a few days in Mulligan's company. The hearty New Yorker was a charter member of the Sons of Liberty, as an English parliamentarian had styled America's militant rebels. Early in 1770 he had participated in the first bloodletting of the Revolution—a skirmish between the Liberty Boys and a coterie of English soldiers on Golden Hill, a section of New York roughly identical with what is now John Street west of William Street. Taking an instant liking to his charge, Mulligan lodged the West Indian in his Water Street home and accompanied him wherever he went. When Alexander resumed his travels it was with the happy knowledge that he had already made one good friend in his adopted country. In the war that was approaching more swiftly than anybody dreamed, Hercules Mulligan was to play a bizarre and adventuresome role, and "my young friend Hamilton," as he habitually referred to Alexander, was to help him play it.

Winter was setting in when in mid-November the pilgrim arrived in the village of Elizabethtown, now Elizabeth, New Jersey. Chill winds had sprinkled the salt meadows with crystal, and the young man from the tropics must have been struck by the contrast between the florid vistas of his Caribbean homeland and the bleak grandeur of naked elms against the steely blue of a northern sky. Stranger still to him were the roaring fires on the hearths of every village home, the hissing of steam from the iron kettles slung above kitchen flames, the way the early frosts made a glassy high-way of the little river running through the town and the early snows altered the contours of the outlying hills.

The Reverend Dr. Knox had supplied his protégé with letters to Elizabethtown's most important residents. One of them was scholarly, middle-aged William Livingston, member of the influential and far-flung Livingston clan. A successful attorney who would rather have been a writer or an artist, Livingston had only recently closed his New York office with the idea of passing his remaining years among his books and paintings in the quiet of the New Jersey country-side. Domiciling his family temporarily in Elizabethtown, he was supervising the erection on the outskirts of a splendid retreat to be known as Liberty Hall, unaware that events would soon call him from retirement to serve his country, first as a delegate to the Continental Congress, later as first governor of the state of New Jersey.

Another letter of introduction carried Alexander to a tall mansard-roofed house, known then as Great House, later as Boxwood Hall. Its proprietor was a rising young attorney named Elias Boudinot. Lawyer Boudinot had not always en-joyed the affluence symbolized by his recent purchase of Great House from its original owner. Like Alexander, he had known poverty in his childhood and had found the solu-tion for it in hard work and voluminous reading. If he him-self answered the traveler's knock that November day, then the stoop of his new house was the starting place of an en-during and mutually valuable friendship. What Alexander saw as he stood there, three-cornered hat in hand, was a stocky, full-faced man of thirty-two, with deep wrinkles in the corners of a mobile mouth. The older man's exploring gaze took in a short, alert youth with snapping dark blue eyes in a fair and slightly freckled face. Even at this early point in his life, something in Alexander Hamilton—perhaps the memory of his trying boyhood in the islands—gave his face, in repose, a somber and clouded look, but his sudden and stabbing smile leaped like a flame in shadow.

The persistent legend that he began his American life as a neglected waif fades before the picture of his years in Elizabethtown. Elias Boudinot made him welcome immediately. Until the Revolution broke out, changing the pattern of life throughout the colonies, Boudinot's home was Alexander's home; Boudinot's family—a wife and two small daughters—his family; and Boudinot himself his shrewd and benevolent counselor, his American Hugh Knox, so to speak. Nor was William Livingston behindhand in kindliness. His house, too, stood open to the immigrant. If Alexander spent a disproportionate amount of time there, it was because the retired attorney's daughters were only slightly older than himself—and a fondness for pretty women was one of his strongest leanings.

The academy selected by his New York mentors was only steps from the Boudinot house. In after years townspeople would recall seeing the diligent youth pacing the adjoining burial ground in the early morning hours, conning his Greek verbs and memorizing his Latin case-endings. It is probably from this phase of his life that the confusion has arisen concerning the still undocumented date of his birth. Finding himself in class with students several years his junior, he did what any sensitive boy would be tempted to do under the circumstances—gave out that he was a couple of years younger than he was.

The academy's hours were long; its youthful master,

Francis Barber, a strict disciplinarian; but for the attractive new scholar, with his ready smile and his talent for gay small-talk, life in the little Jersey capital was never all Greek verbs and Latin nouns. On snowbound winter afternoons there were cozy gatherings at the Livingston hearth, with the young ladies serving a concoction they called "strawberry tea," to hide from their father the fact that it was actually China tea, banned from the homes and lips of all good patriots because it came to America by way of England and bore the hated English tax. There were sleigh rides on starlit winter nights, hunting parties when spring came; and during the warm months that followed, Alexander must now and then have spied the spry and handsome figure of young Aaron Burr, who having just completed his college work at Princeton, was spending the summer in Elizabethtown, staying with his friend Matthew Ogden and sailing his boat along the bays and kills separating the upper New Jersey coast from Staten Island and Manhattan.

Apparently Alexander's prior formal education had been negligible. He seems to have entered the Elizabethtown academy as a first-year student. He wasted no time, racing through a demanding four-year course in approximately nine months. Two of the colonies' four colleges were within easy distance of his new home: the College of New Jersey in the village of Princeton, whose name it would later take; and King's College in New York. His preference was Princeton. It was Hugh Knox's school. Besides, its stalwart president, John Witherspoon, was as incorrigible a rebel as Hercules Mulligan. On the other hand, the head and faculty of King's College were known to be of the pro-British or loyalist faction. To Princeton, therefore, went Alexander, to take his entrance test. Hercules Mulligan went along, to introduce his friend to Witherspoon and to stand by, a mountain of beaming encouragement, while Alexander answered the examination questions and then informed the granite-faced Princeton executive of his desire to enroll as an unclassified student, with the privilege of moving toward his degree as rapidly as his exertions justified. The applicant's learning impressed Witherspoon, but the young man's request to follow an accelerated program did not. Americans, in the opinion of the Scotch-born scholar, were always in such a rush to get where they were going that they scarcely knew where they were when they got there. Alexander must move from class to class in the normal manner or go elsewhere.

Elsewhere he went. Elsewhere, of course, was King's College or, to use its modern name, Columbia, which then occupied a large stone building on the shores of the Hudson, a short walk from St. Paul's Church and Broadway. The authorities of the New York school posed no objections to Alexander's wish to get where he was going in a rush, permitting him to enroll on that basis in the fall of 1773.

That he landed in New York instead of the village of Princeton was just as well. The city's variety and clangor were congenial to his temperament, and he quickly became as much a part of town as of gown by joining one of the volunteer fire companies. As on his previous visit, he lived with Hercules Mulligan, who since their first meeting had acquired a wife and the beginnings of a family. When in his old age the husky merchant penned his reminiscences of "my young friend Hamilton," it pleased him to recall how in the evenings Alexander would join the Mulligans in the living room and entertain them by dashing off bits of humorous verse and reading them aloud.

At Columbia he concentrated on mathematics, "the science of physic" (medicine), natural science, and the classics. On an average day, study and classwork kept him busy from five or six in the morning until eight in the evening. No doubt he would have raced through college as he had raced through the Elizabethtown academy had not events cut short the education he had traveled so far to get.

In 1773 the fuse of war was burning fast. In December a Boston mob dramatized their distaste for English taxes by dumping three boatloads of English tea into the Atlantic. The British Parliament's reaction to the "Boston tea party" was a series of laws further restricting colonial freedoms and known in this country as "the intolerable acts." Among other things, these measures closed the port of Boston, a step unlikely to make loyal British subjects out of the many Boston merchants, shippers, sailors, and mechanics dependent on the port for their livelihoods.

Casting an approving eye on the intolerable acts, King George III blandly informed his prime minister: "the die is now cast; the colonies must either submit or triumph"—a statement that merits attention as an example of that rarest of human utterances, an accurate prophecy. But there was no such word as "submit" in the vocabulary of the Boston patriots. At the suggestion of leaders in Virginia, nearly all of the colonies had organized Committees of Correspondence. Set up to consolidate resistance to what their members regarded as British "tyranny," these committees corresponded regularly, each informing the others of the steps its colony was taking and urging them to do the same. When news of the intolerable acts reached the New World in the spring of 1774, this communications network hummed with schemes for showing the "Mother of Parliaments" the error of her ways.

Rapidly a two-part program emerged. First, each of the colonies was to name delegates to a Continental Congress to meet in Philadelphia during the coming fall. Second, this Congress was to pass a non-importation, non-exportation agreement under which all of the colonies would bind themselves to refrain from trading with England—to sell her little or nothing and to buy little or nothing from her until she reopened the port of Boston.

It would be a gross exaggeration to say that this program drew immediate and universal support. So ringingly has American history celebrated the actions of the patriots of the Revolutionary War, it is easy to forget that to a substantial degree it was a civil war, with Americans often fighting each other with as much if not more animosity than went into the conflict with England itself. Fully a third of the American people refused to abandon their allegiance to the Crown. They remained loyalists or, as the patriots called them, Tories, to the end. Thousands of them joined the English army and navy. Other thousands served the enemy as spies and informers.

On the eve of the Revolution, loyalist sentiment was especially vigorous in New York. There the proposal to refrain from trade with England found the people divided into three camps. At one extreme stood the loyalists, opposed to any action likely to widen the already dangerously wide breach with Britain. At the other extreme were the so-called radicals, consisting of the Sons of Liberty and other warm Whigs. In between were a large number of "Yorkers," who can be best described as conservatives, although "lukewarm Whigs" was the term most often bestowed on them. The majority of New York's businessmen fell into this group. Their commercial ties with the mother country were close, exten-

sive, and profitable. In the proposed ban on trade they detected a threat to their personal fortunes. When war actually
came, most of them would reluctantly side with the colonies.
Meanwhile they favored seeking a reconciliation with King
and Parliament instead of chancing the open break almost
certain to follow the enactment of a non-exportation, non-
importation agreement.

In early June the General Assembly, the colonial legislature, began choosing delegates to the Continental Congress.
Loyalists and lukewarm Whigs dominated the body. When
it became apparent that New York's congressional delegation was going to have a conservative tinge, a howl of disappointment arose among the patriots. To protest the assembly's lack of militancy, the radicals summoned the freemen
or voters of New York City to a giant indignation meeting.
In late June broadsides went up everywhere. These set the
date of the rally for July 7, 1774—and with the loyalists repeatedly demonstrating against the scheduled gathering and
the Liberty Boys counter-demonstrating for it, the city
braced for what people would later call "the great meeting
in the fields."

None of these occurrences escaped the notice of Alexander Hamilton. Born a British subject, he had arrived on
American soil convinced that he would die a British subject.
Gradually, under the influence of Hercules Mulligan and
his friends in New Jersey, he adopted the radical position.
Better the risk of separation from England than submission
to the laws of a Parliament where Americans had no repre-
sentation.

The young West Indian was given to thinking on his feet.
When he had a problem to solve or a paper to write, he
would walk back and forth, talking in an undertone. In Eliz-

abethtown the Presbyterian burial ground had been his thinking site. In New York one of his haunts for this purpose was a stretch of Batteau (now Dey) Street near the college. Back and forth he would go, in the heavy shade of the plane trees; back and forth, talking to himself.

He was thus engaged on the morning of the great meeting in the fields, when he encountered a local radical whose identity has been lost to history. Naturally the two men fell to discussing the quarrel with England. Struck by the younger man's logic and the aptness of his language, the nameless patriot not only suggested that they attend the rally together but that Alexander mount the platform and address the people.

We can readily imagine the startled collegian's response to this proposition: his instant assertion that it would be unbecoming in one so young to do such a thing, the leap of pride within at being asked to do so, the nervousness with which, a few hours later, he did climb onto the platform in the fields. All of the preceding speakers had been older men whose names and faces were familiar to the audience. A murmur rippled from the crowd as nineteen-year-old Alexander appeared. It was the reaction of people puzzled by a new face and dubious about the ability of a mere stripling to illuminate the hard questions of the hour. The murmurs died away as, hesitatingly at first and then more fluently, Hamilton launched into his harangue. When he finished there were cheers. The winds of long ago have carried away whatever he said that afternoon; press accounts of the meeting did not so much as mention his name. All the same, something had happened that future generations would remember. One of the most turbulent, controversial, and constructive public careers in American history had begun.

3

With Pen and Sword

After his speech in the fields, Hamilton was a marked man. The New York radicals hailed him as a useful addition to their ranks. They solicited his friendship; they took him into their councils; they spoke approvingly of his abilities in their letters to one another; and they applauded when during the closing months of 1774 new developments in the quarrel with Britain injected the articulate student still more deeply into the mainstream of his time and place.

In September, as scheduled, the first Continental Congress convened in Philadelphia. In mid-October it passed the long-anticipated non-importation, non-exportation act calling for an almost total boycott on trade with England. To appreciate the reaction of the people of politically divided New York, it is helpful to remember that throughout the fifteen years of its existence the Continental Congress lacked the power to pass laws as such. It could only issue recommendations, leaving it to the people, acting through their local governments, to implement them or not as they chose.

Throughout most of the colonies the response to Congress' first proposal was encouraging. Everywhere committees of enforcement sprang up. In many communities these agencies published in the press the names of people "so far lost to virtue and patriotism" as to disobey "the decrees of the Honorable the Congress." In some areas patriot committees supplemented this procedure by subjecting suspected offenders to such persuasive punishments as house burnings or tar-and-feathering.

But in the province of New York, where the colonial assembly was still preeminently conservative, enforcement was uneven, and the early winter saw the outbreak of a battle of words over whether the people should heed the recommendations of Congress or the laws of Parliament.

Mid-December brought a smashing attack on the non-exportation, non-importation act in the form of a pamphlet entitled "Free Thoughts, on the Proceedings of the Continental Congress." Eighteenth-century political writers often used pen names. The author of "Free Thoughts" signed himself "A. W. Farmer," meaning "A Westchester Farmer." Actually he was no farmer. He was the Reverend Dr. Samuel Seabury, rector of St. Peter's church in Westchester County and the man soon to become America's first Episcopal bishop. Born in Connecticut and educated at Yale, Edinburgh, and Oxford, Seabury at the age of forty-five was the possessor of a trenchant, orderly, and highly trained mind. Throughout the revolutionary period his abilities would make him one of the American loyalists' most eloquent spokesmen.

By the time his "Free Thoughts" appeared, the first Continental Congress had adjourned following a decision to meet again in Philadelphia in May of the coming year. The Westchester cleric accused its members of having "broken up without . . . attempting one step that tended to peace." He called their plea for a ban on trade with England an "abominable scheme" to create an independent and republican America. "Will you submit to them?" he challenged. "By Him that made me, I will not.—No, if I must be enslaved, let it be by a King at least, & not by a parcel of upstart lawless Committee-men. If I must be devoured, let me be devoured by the jaws of a lion, and not *gnawed* to death by rats and vermin."

In the province of New York, patriot sentiment was strongest in the city. Most farmers remained pro-British, not so much out of love of Crown and Parliament as out of the "country bumpkin's" natural dislike for the "city slicker." Cannily, the Westchester minister set out to widen this breach. If the boycott on English goods prevailed, he asked, who would suffer? The farmers, of course. They were the people who had the greatest need for English products. It was they who would have to pay the higher prices that the merchants of New York City would exact as little by little the flow of imports from England and her West Indian possessions choked off. True, the mayor of New York had issued orders regulating prices; but Seabury was certain his farmer readers were too shrewd to put their faith in city ordinances. The greedy merchants would find ways of getting around those. Rather than rely on such people, the farmers would be better off trusting "to the mercy of a Turk."

Seabury wrote a lean hard prose, larded with the colorful expressions of the farm country. His style was appealing, his reasoning close. His arguments drew blood in patriot circles.

Every American radical with literary pretensions reached for his quill pen in an effort to answer them. So comparatively feeble were their efforts, however, that for weeks, as a historian would later remark, it looked as if the "farmer" Tory had plowed under the "city slicker" patriots.

But he hadn't. A sigh of relief swept radical ranks with the appearance on December 5, 1774, of a pamphlet called "A Full Vindication of the Members of Congress." Its author's pen name was "Friend to America." So ably did he cope with Seabury's arguments that speculation as to his identity confined itself to the names of America's most gifted patriots. Some said he must be John Adams. Who other than the Boston patriot had the skill with words and the learning that Friend to America displayed? Some said it was John Jay of New York, another patriot propagandist of more than ordinary ability. Even those who had attended the great meeting in the fields and heard its youngest speaker were genuinely confounded on learning that Friend to America was Alexander Hamilton.

Farmer Seabury, as much a lover of combat as Friend to America Hamilton, was not a man to retreat before a few barbs from a college student. Early in 1775 he renewed his assault with a second pamphlet called "A View of the Controversy." A few weeks later Hamilton counterattacked with "The Farmer Refuted." Another Farmer's pamphlet followed, and two more counterattacks from Hamilton.

Assuming a role he would play throughout life, that of defender of the American businessman, Hamilton struck hard at Seabury's charge that the merchants of New York City would use the boycott on English goods to line their pockets. He noted that Congress had asked them to refrain from profiteering. He predicted that most of them would

bow to Congress' wish. They would do so, he said, not because they were high-minded patriots, more concerned with
country than with profits, but because they were smart. He
credited them with realizing that the English laws that had
closed the port of Boston would make their lives equally un-
bearable unless they joined hands with the patriots. Sound-
ing a theme that runs through all of his writings, Hamilton
declared that "a vast majority of mankind is entirely biased
by motives of self-interest." Businessmen, he reasoned, were
more influenced by self-interest than most groups. It followed that they would find it more advantageous than most
groups not only to support the boycott but to desist from
weakening its effects by charging excessive prices.

Seabury argued that American revolutionary fervor was
much ado about nothing. How could the people of the colonies claim that England was "oppressing" them and keep a
straight face when they said it? All Parliament had done was
to put a tax on tea, a tax so trifling that the price of tea in
America was lower than it was in England. Hamilton handled this line of thought with verve. Give England the right
to put a small tax on one item, and soon she would be putting bigger and bigger taxes on more and more items. "Perhaps before long," he warned his readers, "your tables, and
chairs, and platters, and dishes, and knives and forks, and
every thing else, would be taxed. Nay, I don't know but they
would find means to tax you for every child you got, and for
every kiss your daughters received from their sweethearts;
and, God knows, that would soon ruin you." Ruination by
taxes, he added, "is not the worst you have to fear." From a
Parliament free to make laws for those who had no voice in
it, what "security would you have for your lives? How can
any of you be sure you would have the free enjoyment of
your religion long?"

Seabury urged New Yorkers to ignore the Continental Congress because in the eyes of Parliament that body had no legal existence. Hamilton's answer to this contention was an elaborate exposition of the cornerstone of American revolutionary philosophy—the doctrine of natural law. This doctrine assumed that every human being was born with what Thomas Jefferson would later call "certain unalienable Rights." If his government did not protect him in the exercise of those rights, he had not only the right but the obligation to overthrow that government and replace it with one that would. In advancing this idea, Hamilton borrowed a striking figure of speech from an old friend. Years before, Hugh Knox had told his West Indian congregation, "Our duty is written, as it were, with sunbeams." Asserting that Congress drew its authority from a higher source than Parliament, Hamilton wrote that the "sacred rights of mankind are not to be rummaged for among old parchments or musty records. They are written, as with a sunbeam, in the whole volume of human nature, by the hand of Divinity itself, and can never be erased or obscured by mortal power."

In the Friend to America pamphlets, fifty thousand words in all, Hamilton did not limit himself to answering his adversary's arguments. He ran the gamut of current issues. He doubted that England would go to war. He believed the colonies could gain their ends, simply by standing together and insisting on their liberties. Should there be a war, however, he had some suggestions for conducting it. He pointed out that the colonies had not developed enough industry as yet to support an offensive war. Their wisest course would be to wage a basically defensive one, a war of attrition. American generals should avoid large pitched battles, lest they lose their armies to England's well trained and plentifully supplied troops. They should concentrate on small but frequent harassing attacks, supplemented by numerous retreats aimed at drawing the British invaders into the interior—into areas of the country strange to them but familiar to the Americans. Twenty-year-old Hamilton's presumption in laying out his country's strategy brings a smile. The fact remains that the Fabian tactics he advocated in 1775 were precisely those that Commander-in-Chief George Washington and his generals would pursue.

Although almost certain that no war was coming, the author of the Friend to America pamphlets put his finger on one of the causes of the war that did come. The British, he believed, suffered from "a jealousy of our dawning splendor." A penetrating statement: King George and his ministers sensed that if the colonies were left alone to develop as they wished, they would soon be bigger and richer than the mother country. Most of His Majesty's subjects felt the same way. In England, on the eve of the Revolution, popular support for the King's colonial policies rested on the conviction that "those American peasants" must be kept in their place.

Visible only at scattered points in Hamilton's first important political publication were those beliefs, that in the perspective of time have identified his name with early American conservatism, even as that of his great political rival, Thomas Jefferson, has become identified with the liberalism of the period. The Friend to America pamphlets exhibited several opinions that their author would in time modify, along with some that he would repudiate altogether. At this point in his life he could write that the colonial legislatures should have more power than the Continental Congress, a states' rights position that within a few years he would be combating with every fiber of his passionate being.

To follow the shifts in Alexander Hamilton's thinking, it

is useful to examine some of the political trends at work in the colonies during and right after the revolutionary period. Three theories of government were swimming, as it were, in the American thought stream.

One was democracy. Frankly, few citizens were yet ready for this concept. Aside from Jefferson, only a handful of Americans believed that the will of the majority should prevail. Most of them were convinced that the vote should be qualified, that it should be given only to a man who owned at least a little property.

Another notion, somewhat more widely held, was "benevolent absolutism." The fullest expression of this system had appeared a century before in the works of Thomas Hobbes, an English political writer. Hobbes thought human beings were a mess. He conceded that they were born "free and equal." Unhappily, they were so naturally ornery and so given to fighting one another that unless restrained by a powerful government their lives tended to be "poor, nasty, brutish and short." What was the solution to the problem? In his book *Leviathan,* Hobbes proposed that the people hand over their natural rights to an absolute sovereign, a king or a congress elected for life. He called this government-by-social-contract. Under the terms of his suggested "contract," the absolute sovereign's chief duty would be to protect and tend the welfare of the citizens. The citizens' chief duty would be to obey the sovereign.

Way and above the most widely held theory in revolutionary America was "limited and responsible rule under a constitution." The fullest expression of this theory had appeared in 1690 in what for two centuries was one of the most popular books in the New World, *Two Treatises on Government* by John Locke, another English author. Locke took a kindlier view of human beings. He considered them quite capable of ruling themselves. He advocated, simply as a matter of convenience, that they name representatives to govern for them and with their consent. As a starter he proposed that the people write a constitution. This document, the basic law, should severely limit the powers of the people's representatives. It should also provide for frequent elections. Then when the representatives overstepped their powers or ignored the will of the voters, the people could throw the rascals out.

In the Friend to America tracts, Hamilton leaned a little more toward Locke's limited government than he did toward Hobbes' benevolent absolutism. Later he would lean the other way. That he altered his views from time to time as he grew older is hardly amazing. He had come to America to feed his mind. A fed mind grows, and a growing mind changes.

Even at age twenty he was conservative enough to lament the conduct of patriot extremists. When one brisk spring night a gang of shouting rebels tried to kidnap Myles Cooper, the Tory president of Columbia, Hamilton spirited Cooper from the building and accompanied him to the safety of a friend's home. When, a few months later, another rebel gang demolished the presses of James Rivington, the New York Tory printer, Hamilton wrote a letter of protest to his friend John Jay, then sitting with the New York delegation in the Continental Congress at Philadelphia. The young patriot had nothing but contempt for the "pernicious literature," meaning the pro-loyalist literature, Rivington's press was turning out. In his opinion, however, the way to handle Rivington was for Congress to pass a law forbidding him to publish. Our not-so-liberal young Hamilton was no cham-

pion of a free press. The point of his letter to Jay was that
nobody, patriot or loyalist, had a right to take the law into
his own hands. It is of interest that on this issue Hamilton
and Jefferson had no quarrel. Although the tall, red-headed
Virginia statesman believed that "a little rebellion now and
then is a good thing," he had deplored the violence and property destruction of the Boston tea party. The pleas for order
and for respect for law constantly flowing from the leaders of
the American Revolution are impressive.

Hamilton's *Friend to America* tracts had no immediate
effect on the political situation of his province. Where support of the patriot cause was concerned, New York continued to lag behind most of the other colonies until the outbreak of hostilities at Lexington, Massachusetts, released a
surge of revolutionary ardor. Quickly making the most of
this change, the New York patriots ousted the old colonial
authorities and set up their own governments. Included
among these were a provincial congress to rule the state and
a group of committees that would govern New York City as
long as it remained under American control.

With war a reality, Hamilton was no longer content to
serve the cause with his pen alone. As of April 19, 1775, date
of the skirmish at Lexington, he seems to have been drilling
for several months with a company of volunteers. Now he
began studying artillery, drawn to this branch of the service
presumably because of the mathematical bent of his mind.

In August he experienced his first taste of battle conditions when he and his fellow volunteers received orders from
the local Committee of Safety to seize some cannon the British had installed on the Battery, the parade ground along
the New York waterfront. Hercules Mulligan took part in
this expedition. His written account of it, the fullest one we

have, understates the drama of the incident without obscuring it.

Since a British man-of-war, the *Asia,* was standing out in the harbor, the cannon-stealers chose a dark night for their mission. Unfortunately, some sailors from the *Asia* were patrolling the shore in a small boat. Spotting the Americans at work, they loosed a fusillade of musketry and then made for their ship to give the alarm. At about this point, Hercules Mulligan recalled later, "I was engaged in hawling off one of the cannon when Mr. Hamilton came up." Big and powerful though Mulligan was, he must have been near exhaustion after a long pull northward, straining at the rope slung around his heavy load. At any rate, Hamilton insisted on dragging the cannon the rest of the way. To free his hands he gave his musket to the other man.

Mulligan then returned to the Battery. He was there when the big guns of the *Asia* itself opened fire. In his anxiety to be off, he dropped his friend's musket. He had put the parade ground behind him when he ran into Hamilton, who had moved the cannon to a safe place and was returning to the scene of action. Where was his musket, the young volunteer demanded. Mulligan explained why he had left it on the Battery. "Well," said Hamilton in effect, "if that's where it is, that's where I'm going." And, deaf to the older man's protests and warnings, he proceeded to the waterfront, still alive with exploding balls and grape from the *Asia,* "with as much unconcern," to quote Mulligan, "as if the warship were not there."

Hamilton's actions on the Battery in the summer of 1775 were typical of his conduct throughout the war and indeed throughout life. Both as a soldier and a public official, the future spokesman for his country's most staid and cautious elements was often daring to the point of foolhardiness. He was also bumptious. When in January of 1776, New York's Provincial Congress ordered the establishment of an artillery company, he betook himself at once to the Committee of Safety to request the captaincy of it.

He was twenty-one at this time and still a rosy-cheeked boy in appearance. The members of the committee hesitated. According to Hercules Mulligan, they agreed to give Hamilton a commission only if in the near future he raised at least thirty men for the projected artillery unit. Was this a serious proposition? Or was it the authorities' way of brushing off a brash young man, since they had every reason to question his ability to fulfill the condition? If this was their thinking, they were in for a surprise. Hamilton called on the authorities early in the day. By nightfall, and with Mulligan's help, he had raised twenty-five men. On the following morning the Committee of Safety sent his name to the Provincial Congress, where two months later the secretary recorded that "Alexander Hamilton be and he is hereby appointed Captain of the Provincial Company of Artillery of this Colony."

The fledgling captain had to equip his company out of his own pocket until such time as sufficient money could be deducted from his men's pay. To daring and bumptiousness, add a scarcely surprising touch of vanity. The records show him paying several times more for his own uniform—buckskin breeches and a blue coat with buff cuffs and facings—than for that of his men.

One of his earliest official acts was a defiance of military tradition. When a lieutenant was promoted out of his company, Hamilton persuaded the Provincial Congress to replace him by commissioning one of the sergeants. Probably the first such promotion from the ranks of modern times, this development started a trend. Impressed by the competence of the sergeant-turned-lieutenant, the New York legislators passed a resolution encouraging commanders in the provincial militia to lift to officer rank "from time to time such privates and non-Commissioned Officers . . . as shall distinguish themselves by their Sobriety, Valour, and Subordination."

Hamilton was diligent in training his troops and in discouraging them from the practice common to all soldiers of resorting to such inelegant expletives as "tarnation!" and "damn my wig!" Hercules Mulligan noted with avuncular pride that the captain took good care of his troops. He got them a raise in pay. He saw that their quarters were clean and their meals ample. He visited the sick in person. The big merchant's observations underscore another of his young friend's characteristics. It would be said of Hamilton later that he loved his country more than he loved his countrymen. A just enough appraisal, for the day was near when he would regard mankind-in-the-mass with a jaundiced eye; but to those individuals who actually crossed his path—friends, near friends, even casual acquaintances—he tended to be considerate and kind, often self-sacrificingly so.

By the time he made captain, the conflict that had opened with a skirmish at Lexington had become full-scale war. Every colony had activated its militia. The Congress in Philadelphia had established the Continental Army with George Washington as commander-in-chief. The Battle of Bunker Hill, the capture of Fort Ticonderoga, the attempt to storm Quebec, the siege of British-held Boston—these and several lesser confrontations had already become historic milestones.

When early in 1776 the British abandoned Boston, Washington moved his army from Cambridge, Massachusetts, to Manhattan. During the spring and summer his twenty thousand troops hastily threw up earthworks in the city and on nearby Long Island, stretched a 2,100-foot chain across the lower Hudson, placed a line of sunken ships, held together by chains, farther up—about where the George Washington Bridge now spans the river—and installed a gauntlet of batteries on its high banks. Hamilton and his men guarded the provincial records and helped construct Bayard's Hill Redoubt, a small fort on what is now the intersection of Canal and Mulberry streets.

These efforts to keep New York City in American hands were doomed from the beginning. The colonies had no navy to pit against the "ruler of the waves." Neither in numbers nor in training were Washington's green troops a match for the expeditionary force that King George and Parliament were rushing to the assistance of Sir William Howe, the British commander in America.

In July the New York harbor was a forest of white sails, with 52 enemy warships and 427 troop transports riding its swells. On Staten Island, 34,000 redcoats grumbled at the size of the mosquitoes and shivered under thin blankets during a series of rainstorms. With the coming of better weather, 14,000 of them swarmed onto the southern beaches of Brooklyn. The ensuing battle—the Battle of Long Island —on August 27 forced 7,000 American soldiers to take refuge behind a row of flimsy fortifications on Brooklyn Heights. Two days later, in the dark of night, Washington contrived to bring them across the East River to Manhattan, literally snatching them from under the noses of their potential captors. This was a masterly maneuver. It saved a third of Washington's army—but it did not save New York. Shortly before noon, September 15, the British landed in force at Kip's Bay, an inlet of the East River at the end of what would later be Thirty-fourth Street.

Some twenty-four hours earlier, Washington had reluctantly concluded that the city could not be held. When the British landed, his army was in full retreat. Most of the troops were safely above the Thirty-fourth Street line—but a few small contingents, Captain Hamilton's company among them, found themselves trapped south of the line at Bayard's Hill Redoubt. The officers and men of the fort were making preparations to defend it to the bitter end when a young American major suddenly reined in his horse at the outworks of the compound and announced that he brought good news.

It would appear that it was at this moment and under these hectic circumstances that Alexander Hamilton and Aaron Burr came face to face for the first time. The major— Burr—said that it was still possible to move up the island without encountering the invaders. Friends of his, a family named Clarke, lived in Chelsea on the shores of the Hudson River. Coming and going from their home, Burr had become well acquainted with the little-traveled forest paths and wagon roads of western Manhattan. He was certain he could guide the stranded troops to safety. He proved as good as his word. By nightfall the refugees from Bayard's Hill Redoubt had reached Harlem Heights where, on Washington's orders, the fleeing army had halted and was digging in.

At the Battle of Harlem Heights on the following day, the Americans gave a good account of themselves. But standing off the enemy in the buckwheat fields of Harlem was not in itself sufficient to break the British hold on Manhattan.

Other engagements followed—in upper Manhattan, in Westchester County, and on the western shores of the Hudson—until Washington, fearful of losing his army, crossed the Passaic River on November 20 and began his seven-week retreat south and west across New Jersey.

Sir William Howe and his army pursued, and in accounts written then or fairly soon after, we catch three glimpses of Captain Hamilton and his artillerists at work. At New Brunswick his battery helped delay the English long enough to permit Washington to push on toward Philadelphia. At Princeton, Hamilton himself seems to have fired the cannon that emptied the college building Nassau Hall of redcoats, and, according to an English authority, put a ball through the college's painting of a one-time occupant of the British throne, King George II. And when on Christmas night, 1776, Washington's surprise attack on Trenton blunted the English advance and saved Philadelphia for the time being, Hamilton and his soldiers, their guns strategically placed, cleared a Trenton street of the Hessian mercenaries King George III had hired to help chastise "those American peasants."

Just when and how the eyes of George Washington fell approvingly on artillery captain Hamilton is one of those mysteries history delights in dangling before us. Perhaps Washington had read the Friend to America pamphlets and so was aware of Hamilton's felicity with the pen. A creditable story is that Nathanael Greene, one of Washington's ablest generals, was impressed by Hamilton's military diligence and called him to the attention of the commanding general. Another has it that, at Harlem Heights, Washington himself was so taken with Hamilton's conduct that he then and there invited the young West Indian to his marquee.

There are other versions, none verified, all plausible. Whatever the course of this development, it came to a head soon after the American army retired to winter quarters at Morristown, New Jersey. On March 1, 1776, general orders for the day made Hamilton an aide-de-camp and a secretary to the commander-in-chief with the rank of lieutenant colonel, a step tantamount to placing him on the first rung of the ladder he would climb to the glories and the miseries of fame.

4

The Little Lion

Hamilton's assignment to the staff of the commander-in-chief in the spring of 1777 lifted him from the obscurity of a small militia command to the fiercely limelighted world of great affairs where he would spend the rest of his life. Geographically, the headquarters of the Continental Army moved as the war moved. But wherever it went, all of the problems of the conflict followed. The commander-in-chief's secretarial staff was small—thirty-two aides in all during the seven years of the war, with seldom more than six or seven on duty at one time—but its labors were huge. If Washington placed heavy burdens on his aides, it was because his own were staggering. There was a raw new army to be whipped into a disciplined force. There were the multiple elements of a military machine to be organized—supply department, intelligence department, hospital system. There were delicate relations to be maintained with a Congress uncertain of its powers but jealous of its prerogatives, with the legislatures of thirteen sovereign states, and with such foreign allies—chiefly France and Spain—as could be persuaded to support a barely viable nation. Whether headquarters was an inn, a home, a tent on the battlefield or along the line of march, or simply the backs of saddled horses, the work of directing intricate and far-flung operations went relentlessly on.

"It is absolutely necessary," Washington remarked of his aides, "for me to have persons that can think for me as well as execute orders." In Hamilton the overworked general found an assistant so extraordinarily skilled on both scores that a familiar sound at headquarters, whenever a serious problem arose, was the voice of the tall, bulky commander-in-chief bellowing, "Call Colonel Hamilton!"

Washington's reliance on Hamilton would not end with the war. It would continue, with only one small rift, throughout the younger man's life. In one respect their collaboration was a strange one. There is no evidence that the general was ever more than mildly fond of the West Indian. There is every evidence that Hamilton did not like the older man at all. After three years at headquarters, Hamilton would confess, "I have felt no friendship for him [Washington] and have professed none. The truth is, our dispositions are the opposites of each other, and the pride of my temper would not suffer me to profess what I did not feel."

The chain that bound the two men was a combination of mutual respect and need. Washington admired and made use of Hamilton's talents, especially of his writing talents. During the war Hamilton recognized the general's importance as a national symbol, the one man capable of unifying diverse American interests and maintaining the union. Later he would value the prestige that Washington alone could shed on his—Hamilton's—views of how that union should develop. The very lukewarmness of their alliance lent objectivity to Washington's always generous appraisals of his collaborator. In a letter to John Adams he noted that some people considered Hamilton "an ambitious man, & therefore a dangerous one; that he is ambitious I shall readily grant, but it is of the laudable kind that prompts a man to excell in whatever he takes in hand."

The degree to which Hamilton excelled as a military secretary owed much to inborn genius. It also owed something to the circumstances of his birth and early rearing. "I am a stranger in this country," he confided to his fellow secretary, handsome John Laurens of South Carolina. "I have no property here, no connections." Laurens and most of the other aides-de-camp belonged to established American families. Save for his friends in Elizabethtown and New York, the headquarters "family," as Washington invariably spoke of his staff, was all the family Hamilton had. The other aides could look forward to assured positions once the war ended. If he were to have a future in America, he must earn it now. Earn it he did. He won the approval of his fellow aides by the superior quality of his work, their affection by the sunniness of his manner.

Their letters testify to their pleasure in his "sparkling conversation," his "ease, propriety and vivacity." They smiled when he vetoed a scheme to kidnap the British general, Sir Henry Clinton, with the argument that Clinton should be left where he was because his incompetence was one of the enemy's greatest liabilities. They chuckled when, in a letter to Brigadier General Anthony Wayne, he recommended an applicant for a chaplaincy with the statement that the minister in question had no shortcomings "except that he does not drink and will not insist on your going to Heaven whether you want to or not." They viewed with jealous admiration his repeated success with the young ladies whose occasional visits at headquarters relieved the tedium of the daily grind. Cheerful James McHenry of Maryland described himself as "never so taken aback" as when, during a stay at a riverside tavern, the "pretty milk maids" of the establishment showed more interest in the members of Washington's Life Guard (his special body-guard) than in "swashbuckling Hamilton."

When Dr. McHenry joined the staff, he vowed never to return to the practice of medicine. For his "swashbuckling" friend, however, he made an exception. Attributing a slight indisposition to overindulgence in wine, he prescribed a "table of diet" that he predicted would not only relieve Hamilton's symptoms but "have a tendency also to correct your wit." When Congress selected John Laurens for a delicate foreign mission, the earnest South Carolinian protested that the delegates had picked the wrong man. He insisted that the talents of "my dear Hammy" were far superior to his own. Only Laurens and McHenry seem to have used the nickname "Hammy." It was sobersided Robert Hanson Harrison, Washington's chief secretary, who fondly bestowed on Hamilton the nickname posterity would remember: "The Little Lion."

For the commander-in-chief the Little Lion performed a variety of services. He helped him with his voluminous correspondence. Washington had little time for actual dictation. In common with the other aides, Hamilton had to

compose most of his letters with little to go on but a grunted
hint or two from his chief, often not even that. He traveled
widely, functioning as a "trouble-shooter." He participated
in councils of war, where his suggestions and opinions were
welcomed. He represented Washington in negotiations with
the British over the exchange of military prisoners. This was
vexing work since the British regularly disregarded the rules
of war on the ground that the Americans were not an
"enemy" in the normal sense, but a pack of outlaws engaged
in treasonable activities against their king. He handled much
of the general's intelligence work. It was in this connection
that he one day introduced his friend, Hercules Mulligan, to
Washington. Espionage activities do not find their way into
military records. We know, however, that from this moment
on Mulligan was one of the most active American spies in
British-occupied New York City.

Hamilton's early months at headquarters coincided with
the opening by the British of a two-pronged campaign
aimed at smashing the rebellion without further ado. From
Canada, the British dramatist-general, "Gentleman"
Johnny Burgoyne, led six thousand men southward in an
effort to divide New York State from New England by
snatching control of the Hudson River valley. Simultane-
ously the British commander-in-chief in America, Sir William Howe, embarked at New York with an even larger
army. He too traveled south, landing his troops at the head
of Chesapeake Bay and then moving them eastward toward
Philadelphia.

Howe's major objective was not seizure of the Quaker
City. He hoped that Washington, alarmed by a threat to the

rebel "capital," would meet the advancing British in open warfare and lose his army. The engagement did occur, but although the Battle of the Brandywine on September 11, 1777, was a resounding American defeat, Washington succeeded in withdrawing with his battered army intact. From the shores of the Brandywine, a small creek in southeast Pennsylvania, the British marched on, gradually closing in on the city from the west.

During this feverish period, aide-de-camp Hamilton put aside his secretarial quill. On a blustery September morning he and Captain Richard Henry Lee of Virginia took a body of horse to a tiny settlement on the banks of the Schuylkill, across river from the wooded suburbs of Philadelphia. Their orders were to destroy flour stored in the mills there before the enemy reached the area. They had barely accomplished their task when shots from their outposts warned them of the sudden arrival of a British detachment.

Hamilton and four of the dragoons rode their horses onto a flatboat that Hamilton had foresightedly tied up at the river bank. As they pulled hard up-stream under a volley of musketry, one of their number was killed. The rest of them might have been had not Captain Lee drawn off some of the enemy fire by mounting his horse and galloping away in a different direction.

That night Hamilton dispatched an express rider to Philadelphia with a message for John Hancock, president of Congress. If the members of that body had "not yet left Philadelphia," he wrote, "they ought to do it immediately." The Congressmen evinced no reluctance about acting on this suggestion. Indeed, the portly member from Massachusetts, John Adams, took off at once and unencumbered by company. Taking a prudently roundabout course through New

Jersey, he rejoined his fellow delegates at Lancaster, Pennsylvania, where he sprinkled his diary with vitriolic criticisms of Colonel Hamilton for having scared Congress into "undignified flight" before a single redcoat had crossed the Schuylkill. No objections were heard from the Boston statesman, however, when after one brief session in Lancaster, the delegates voted to put still more space between themselves and the endangered city, and hustled across the Susquehanna River to the little town of York on the Pennsylvania frontier.

With or without dignity, all Congressmen had left the city by the evening of September 19. A week later the British tramped in.

An attempt by Washington to dislodge them on October 4 ended in failure. In his analysis for Congress of the Battle of Germantown, Hamilton attributed the American defeat to "hazy weather." His report would have been more accurate had he mentioned the superior timing and tactics of the British. Any number of Fourth of July orations to the contrary, the officers and soldiers sent across the Atlantic by King George were second to none in discipline and valor. On the battlefield the American soldiers enjoyed only one consistent advantage: they were better shots. This was partly because they had a more accurate musket, chiefly because, being largely farmers and woodsmen, they had a better eye. A running joke around American campfires was that the average redcoat "couldn't hit a barn from the inside."

At Whitpain, the Americans' temporary camp a few miles from the city, Washington coped with the gloom prevailing after two major defeats in a row and put sharp questions to his general officers. Could Sir William Howe consolidate his position in Philadelphia? The only route available to the

British general for bringing in supplies and reinforcements was the Delaware River, and guarding the river below Philadelphia were two small American forts. These Howe must reduce quickly, or face starvation. Should Washington wait, hoping that the forts would hold; or should he risk annihilation of his army at the hands of a superior force by attacking the city? Headquarters was a buzz of agitated discussion when toward the end of October a messenger arrived with stunning information. Earlier that month at Saratoga, New York, an American army under Major General Horatio Gates had not only halted "Gentleman" Johnny Burgoyne's invasion from Canada, but had captured the elegant English commander and his entire army!

To grasp what this turning point of the war meant to Washington, hovering on the outskirts of British-occupied Philadelphia, requires a glance at some of the complexities of the Revolution. Slight, bespectacled, professorial-looking Horatio Gates, the forty-nine-year-old "hero of Saratoga," was basically an unassuming man. The outpouring of praise for his defeat of Burgoyne, however, would have addled an even steadier head than his. Temporarily smitten with delusions of grandeur, he did not even bother to send the report of his success to his commander-in-chief. He sent it to Congress, who forwarded it to Washington.

The slight did not go unheeded. Washington's hurt feelings, however, did not blind him to the favorable effect that Gates' victory could have on his own position. A few days after verification of the event reached Whitpain, he summoned his generals to a council of war. Together they canvassed their situation on the rim of Philadelphia in the light of the changed situation in upstate New York. For an attack on Howe, Washington must have more soldiers. Where better could he get them than from Gates who, now that Burgoyne was out of the way, no longer needed all of his large army? All those at the conference, including Hamilton—on hand to record the proceedings—knew that obtaining reinforcements from Gates might not be easy. After two disastrous setbacks in a row, Washington's reputation was at low ebb. For the moment, on the other hand, Gates was the darling of the country. If he resisted giving up some of his troops and submitted his objections to Congress, chances were the delegates would support him as against his superior.

Here was a ticklish situation—especially for the man whom the commander-in-chief chose as his emissary to General Gates. Hamilton was his choice. That Washington selected the youngest of his aides for this difficult mission shows that even at this early date their lifelong collaboration was cemented.

Hamilton left headquarters on October 30. A week later he reached his destination to find himself playing shuttlecock in a crossfire of egos as lively as any skirmish on the battlefield. His instructions from Washington were so loosely written that he was practically on his own. Should he present Washington's orders and demand the two brigades that the commander-in-chief wanted, or should he pocket the orders, speak softly to Gates, and get what he could? At military installations along his route, the worried emissary had uncovered what he believed to be the answer to this question. Gates was even more popular than Hamilton had supposed. Taking a high hand with him might create serious problems for Washington. A respectful request appeared to be the wiser course.

He talked with Gates in Albany, where the general had

brought his army following Burgoyne's surrender. Gates demurred at giving up two of his three brigades. He pointed out that he had already sent a rifle detachment to Washington, that he needed a large force in Albany to guard "the finest arsenal in America." He reminded Hamilton that small enemy units were still active in the region. Besides, the commander of the British troops in New York City, Sir Henry Clinton, might one of these days take it into his head to move north. A single brigade, Gates announced, was all that he could spare.

Hamilton accepted it, only to discover within a few days that the unit Gates had chosen was so undermanned as to amount to little more than half a brigade. Angered at what he took to be an act of bad faith, he called again on the hero of Saratoga. This time he made no requests. He produced his orders from Washington and demanded. Caught in an attempt to palm off an undermanned unit on his military superior, Gates submitted to what he later grumpily described as "dictatorial power" exercised by "one Aid de Camp sent to an Army 300 miles distant."

Having obtained his two brigades, Hamilton was about to follow them south when he learned that instead of heading straight for Pennsylvania, both units had halted at Peekskill, New York, where Major General Israel Putnam was in the process of commandeering them for *his* army.

The weatherbeaten old farmer from the rocky fields of Connecticut had a scheme, a "hobby horse" as Hamilton called it. He was dreaming of striking south and attacking Sir Henry Clinton at Manhattan. For this ambitious project, never attempted, a couple of extra brigades would come in handy.

Hamilton called on Putnam. More plain talk—laced, no

doubt, with a little back-country profanity from the gnarled old general as he reluctantly acceded to the demands of Washington's "dictatorial" aide.

But Hamilton's troubles were not over. He was recovering from a bout of fever, brought on by his exertions, when he discovered that his reinforcements were on the brink of mutiny. The soldiers had strong provocation. Their pay was in arrears. Some had not received so much as a shilling for eight months. Hamilton literally leaped from his sickbed. With the help of the governor of New York, he borrowed enough to pay off the troops, and dispatched them south.

The ironic last act of this comedy of frustration took place on the outskirts of Philadelphia. By the time Hamilton reached headquarters with his two brigades, the scheme that had sent him galloping northward—an attack on the city— was no longer feasible. Sir William Howe had demolished the American forts along the lower Delaware River and had received substantial reinforcements from Sir Henry Clinton. Gingerly Washington prodded at the string of redoubts Howe had thrown up around the city. Satisfied that they were too strong even for his now enlarged contingent, he broke camp in late December and led his army into winter quarters, some twenty-five miles northwest of Philadelphia, at Valley Forge.

The American Revolution has been called the most literate war in history. Indeed Julius Caesar's account of his conquest of all Gaul, his *Commentaries,* is thin gruel alongside some of the diaries turned out in droves by Continental soldiers and militiamen ranging in rank from drummer boy to general. Even in the icy winds at Valley Forge the diary-keepers plied their nubby pencils and worn quill pens. It is upon their curiously spelled, seldom grammatical, but unfailingly colorful efforts that historians have erected their picture of that dismal winter: of guards walking lonely posts, their shoeless feet wrapped in tattered blankets; of airless huts filled with acrid smoke of green wood burning on ramshackle hearths; of log hospitals crowded with men dying of hunger and exposure, of bodies lying in shallow trenches in fields too deeply frozen to permit the preparation of proper graves; of, as one exasperated camp doctor lamented, "Poor food—hard lodging—Cold weather—fatigue—Nasty Cloaths—Hasty Cookery—Vomit half my time—smoaked out of my senses—the Devil's in't."

But from these journals comes another and more bearable picture: of a patchwork army composed of Continentals and assorted militia, gradually molded by shared sufferings into a proud and cohesive striking arm. Like all good commanders, Washington saw to it that his soldiers were never idle. At Valley Forge his chief assistant in this morale-building endeavor was the Baron Frederick William August von Steuben, whose arrival at headquarters in February of 1778 was a happy day for the American cause.

A German soldier of fortune, von Steuben had come to the New World bearing letters of introduction to Congress, one of them signed by Benjamin Franklin and attesting to von Steuben's long service as a "Lieut. Gen." in the "army of the King of Prussia." Congress, impressed, accepted von Steuben's offer to serve in the Continental Army without rank or pay. Only later did the Baron confide to Alexander Hamilton that his highest rank in the "army of the King of Prussia" had been a captaincy. By the time this fact had become general knowledge, few Americans cared, having long since found reason to be grateful to the lovable German. As Washington's drillmaster at Valley Forge, von Steuben transformed a ragtaggle army into as smartly stepping a body of soldiery as England herself could place on review.

Hamilton loved the Baron. He derived endless amusement from what he affectionately described as the corpulent German's "fondness for importance." Years later he would be one of the men instrumental in persuading a government, prone in peacetime to forget its wartime heroes, to provide von Steuben with a comfortably financed old age. When Hamilton could get away from his secretarial desk at Valley Forge, nothing relaxed him more than to watch the ebullient drillmaster putting his awkward squads through their paces. Swathed in a gold and scarlet uniform, a mammoth silver star on his chest, von Steuben ranted and scolded at his ill-clad charges. He spoke German, Russian, and French, but since his English was nonexistent, he assigned to his French-speaking assistant, Captain Benjamin Walker, the task of swearing for him in English. *"Viens, Walker, mon ami, mon bon ami! sacré!"* he would roar, looking to the Captain to provide an adequate translation. "Damn *de gaucheries* of dese *badauts. Je ne puis plus.* I can curse them no more."

To the soldiers at Valley Forge the spring of 1778 was more than a welcome return of sap to the tall trees and of warmth and suppleness to the rolling earth. It was a period of hopeful developments. Since the early months of the war France had been secretly helping the Americans. In the winter of 1778 she became an open ally, signing a treaty to this effect and agreeing to send a fleet of warships and perhaps a fighting division or two across the sea. When this news reached the camp along the Schuylkill, the shouts of joy rolling up the surrounding hills were probably audible to the British pickets on the distant outskirts of Philadelphia.

In another sense they were deafeningly heard in the city itself. There the situation had recently undergone one change and was about to undergo another. Sir William Howe had resigned as supreme commander of His Majesty's armies in America and had returned to England. His successor, reaching the Quaker City in May, was Sir Henry Clinton. Short and pudgy, his little eyes nesting in rolls of flesh, the new British leader was a man of spectacular cautiousness. Word that powerful France was sending military aid to the Americans troubled him profoundly. It meant that he would soon be facing a stronger enemy with his own forces divided, some in Philadelphia, some in New York. His timorous mind told him to evacuate the rebel capital and to concentrate his soldiers behind the stronger ramparts of Manhattan Island. When on June 18 he marched out of the city, preceded by a baggage train twelve miles long and followed by the army that had occupied Philadelphia for nine months, Washington and his troops left Valley Forge.

☆   ☆   ☆

Two years before, Sir William Howe had chased the American commander across New Jersey, going south. Now Washington chased Howe's successor across New Jersey, going north. At a tiny settlement then called Monmouth Court House, now Freehold, the two armies intersected.

To gaunt, hawk-nosed, middle-aged Major General Charles Lee, a resident of Virginia but no relation to that state's famous Lee family, Washington gave the task of leading the main American attack. It was an unfortunate choice. Lee had only recently rejoined the Continental Army after eighteen months as a prisoner-of-war. Perhaps capture by the British had diluted his revolutionary ardor, if he in fact possessed any. Perhaps—and his often erratic behavior leans hard toward this assumption—he was a victim of mental illness. No sooner had he launched his assault than, for no apparent reason, he ordered a retreat.

In a swift and masterly maneuver, Washington turned Lee's fleeing soldiers around. As a result, the Battle of Monmouth, in the blistering heat of June 28, 1778, was an American victory, with the enemy losing twelve hundred men—some two hundred dead, the rest deserters. More precisely, it was a partial victory, since it did not prevent Clinton and his reduced but still formidable army from reaching the haven of British-held New York City. The hostilities at Monmouth ceased at sundown. During the night, while the exhausted Americans slept, the British stole away.

At Monmouth, as on the eve of the occupation of Philadelphia, Hamilton dropped his pen to become a field soldier. For four days prior to the battle he was almost ceaselessly on horseback. Serving as a liaison officer, he gathered and distributed intelligence among the elements of Washington's army. During the actual fighting he helped re-form one of Lee's retreating brigades, and suffered a slight but temporarily incapacitating injury when his horse fell dead beneath him.

Militarily the fray on the scorched plains of eastern New Jersey completed a cycle begun in upstate New York. At his headquarters in Manhattan, Sir Henry Clinton brooded on the immediate past: the capture of Burgoyne at Saratoga, his own near-capture at Monmouth. Taken together, these events convinced him that Great Britain could not win the war in the north. Her only chance lay in the southern states, where he had reason to believe loyalist sentiment was high and American military units scattered and weak.

Accordingly he shortly embarked southward to instigate a string of campaigns that for some two years would give England a shaky control over Georgia and the Carolinas. While Sir Henry busied himself in this manner, France made good on her promise to send a fleet to the assistance of the Americans. Its leader, Vice Admiral Charles Hector, Count d'Estaing, was a man of boundless goodwill. Hamilton, frequently boarding his flagship with messages from Washington, got the impression that he was also an able one. Able he may have been but, so far as the patriot cause was concerned, ineffective. Although d'Estaing put in at ports all up and down the Atlantic coast, he accomplished little. Finally, he simply sailed away.

In the north, during this fretful period, something close to a stalemate prevailed. Leaving other generals to do battle in Georgia and the Carolinas, Sir Henry Clinton returned to New York and brooded some more. Like the wife of Ulysses, weaving her shroud by day and unraveling it by night, he made plans and then he unmade them. Once he sallied forth from the city with an army, seemingly bent on some great adventure in New England or in the Hudson River highlands, only shortly to think better of it and scuttle back to the comfort and security of his island fortress. Washington shifted restlessly from place to place, keeping an eye on Sir Henry. Occasionally he garnered a small victory, but for the most part he played a patient waiting game, the only course open to him until France decided to give him further, and hopefully more effectual, aid.

In the winter of 1778–79 the American commander's headquarters were at Middlebrook, New Jersey, a few miles west of Newark. During this period Hamilton was often away, acting as a messenger between Washington and the Count d'Estaing, his fluency in the French admiral's language making him the ideal man for this mission. Whenever he was at headquarters, he helped his friend, John Laurens, draw up a plan for the raising of Negro regiments.

Member of a distinguished South Carolina family—his father was one of the presidents of Congress—John Laurens was only a year or so older than Hamilton: a slender, lithe young man and "every inch the southern Cavalier," to quote an admiring contemporary. Fated to die under fire during a small mopping-up action in the closing weeks of the war, he was the Sir Galahad of the Revolution. Hamilton, no indifferent supporter of the cause himself, marveled at the intensity and selflessness of his friend's patriotism.

Among the officers at headquarters, he alone was sympathetic with Laurens' determination to bring Negroes into the army. On the issue of slavery, then legal in all states, Hamilton was far more liberal than many of the men who in the years to come would denounce him as a reactionary. He viewed any form of human bondage as immoral. He did not agree with Thomas Jefferson, who almost at this same time was expressing the conviction that whites were inherently superior to Negroes. "The contempt we have been taught to entertain for the blacks," Hamilton said, "makes us fancy many things that are founded neither in reason nor experience." He predicted that, were Negroes given equal opportunity, "their natural abilities" would prove to be "as good as ours." In Laurens' scheme—really his and Laurens' scheme—he detected a way to give some of them that opportunity. The scheme envisaged a Negro levy in every state. Congress was to supply the money, slaveholders were to donate the recruits, and those who enlisted were to receive their freedom. Laurens devoted considerable thought to the subject of an appropriate uniform: "white with red facings"— those colors, he assured Hamilton, "would contrast splendidly with dark skins."

When the British seized Georgia and threatened South Carolina, Laurens obtained permission to leave headquarters to fight for his state. En route south in the spring of 1779, he stopped at Philadelphia, now again the American capital, to lay before Congress the plan that he had drafted with Hamilton's help. The delegates listened attentively and passed a resolution, recommending that the states act on Laurens' idea. Some responded affirmatively, notably Rhode Island, whose Negro regiment was to become one of the crack outfits of the war; some would not respond at all as young Laurens soon and sorrowfully discovered.

His appearance in July before the South Carolina assembly was an ordeal. The plantation-owning legislators rejected, with what he described as "contemptuous huzzas," his proposal that they release some of their slaves to the army. In a report to Hamilton, he confessed that the "wound to my spirit" during the encounter with his home legislature was harder to endure than the "wound to my body," suffered a short time before while fighting for his commonwealth.

Winter headquarters in 1779–80 were at Morristown, New Jersey, where Washington and his "family" occupied an English colonial-style house belonging to Mrs. Theodosia Ford, widow of a wealthy ironmaker. In late December, Martha Washington arrived to be with her "old man," as she called the commander-in-chief. It was her custom to join him at the opening of the winter season and leave a few months later when the army marched off to do its summer fighting. "I heard the closing and opening guns of every campaign," she would recall after the war.

Other officers' wives were at headquarters that blizzard-stricken winter. They and a number of young ladies living in the vicinity patriotically defied the snowdrifts to attend the dances that sometimes filled the commissariat storehouse with the cry of fiddles (playing the popular ballad "A Successful Campaign") and the scuffle of the Virginia Reel. Hamilton was often present at these "pretty little frisks," and at one or another of them the swashbuckling aide who hitherto had been lightly interested in many young women became seriously interested in one.

5

Love, Economics, and Glory

If Hamilton's objective in paying court to twenty-two-year-old Elizabeth Schuyler was to rectify the lack of influential "connections" he had mentioned to John Laurens, he could scarcely have chosen better. "Betsey," as everyone called her, was the second-oldest of the eight children of Major General Philip John Schuyler, the leading "patroon" or squire of the upper Hudson River valley. The riverside mansion the patroon had built for his family was the showplace of Albany. His properties were numerous, his business interests ramified and prosperous. Frequently crippled by rheumatic gout, he himself was tall and powerfully built, with a large, almost bulbous nose and piercing eyes. Some read chill arrogance into his courtly manner and stylish clothes. As a matter of fact General Schuyler was an exceptionally sensitive man, capable of deep and lasting affections.

During the first year of the Revolution he had commanded the Northern Department of the Continental Army. Then in 1776 the garrison of a fort in his military district surrendered to the British without a fight, and Congress relieved him of his post and gave it to General Horatio Gates. The subsequent action of a court martial, clearing him of a charge of negligence, failed to salve his wounded pride. Resigning his commission, he retired to his Albany estate, to grumble at his country's ingratitude and to watch with envy while the man who had supplanted him as commander of the Northern Department went on to become the hero of Saratoga.

Naturally he was delighted to chat with a disgruntled young colonel, fresh from a bruising encounter with Gates, when in the autumn of 1777 Alexander Hamilton paid him a courtesy call at Albany. Their brief conversation initiated a lifelong friendship that to the younger man would be nearly as valuable and far more emotionally satisfying than his collaboration with Washington. He and the patroon had much in common: a deep dislike of Horatio Gates, a similar political outlook, and, probably most compelling of all, a shared interest and skill in the science of mathematics.

Whether in 1777 they also had Betsey in common is problematic. Some historians assume that the courtship began during Hamilton's first visit to the Schuylers' yellow-brick homestead, with its baronial ballroom and richly tapestried drawing rooms. A novelist pictures the debonair young aide, while waiting at the foot of the stairs to be summoned, suddenly looking up to behold tomboy Betsey descending from the second floor, straddle-fashion and petticoats flying, on the polished runner of the balustrade. A beguiling version of boy-meets-girl, but a dubious one. It would appear from one of Hamilton's letters that the patroon neglected to introduce him to his womenfolk at that time. One of his fellow aides had already mentioned Betsey's "lively dark eyes" and "natural charm," but he was not to see the eyes or enjoy the charm until three years later when, in the winter of 1780, Betsey traveled south to visit a relative living near Washington's headquarters in Morristown.

Hamilton conducted his romance as he did everything else—with diligence, concentration, and dispatch. They became engaged in March. At this point General Schuyler was also in Morristown, and shortly before or after the engagement, Hamilton spoke to him privately of something he rarely discussed—his illegitimate birth. Far from taking alarm, the proud patroon saw in the young man's honesty further evidence, as he would say later, that in making Betsey his wife, "Alexander Hamilton did honor to the Schuyler family."

They were married in Albany on December 14, 1780. Although slender, delicate, and of medium height, with a satiny complexion and a smooth broad brow, Betsey was no beauty. If in all other respects, however, she came even close to Hamilton's ideal of womanhood, she was forbiddingly perfect. Two years earlier he had listed for John Laurens the qualities he required in a wife. She must be

> . . . Sensible (a little learning will do)—well bred
> . . . chaste and tender . . . of some good nature—a great deal of generosity (she must neither love money nor scolding, for I dislike equally a termagant and an oeconomist)—In politics, I am indifferent what side she may be of. . . . As to religion a moderate stock will satisfy me—She must believe in god and hate a saint. But as to fortune, the larger stock of that the better. . . .

Though I run no risk of going to Purgatory for my ava-
rice, yet as money is an essential ingredient to happiness
in this world—as I have not much of my own—and as I
am very little calculated to get more . . . , it must
needs be that my wife . . . bring at least a sufficiency to
administer to her own extravagancies.

Later Hamilton had second thoughts about the virtue of
"a little learning." In one of his many glowing letters to "my
charmer," he entreated Betsey "not to neglect the charges I
gave you . . . of employing all of your leisure time in reading. . . . You excel most of your sex in all the amiable
qualities, endeavor to excel them equally in the splendid
ones. You can do it if you please. & I shall take pride in it,—
It will be a fund too to diversify our enjoyment & amuse-
ments & fill all our moments to advantage."

Betsey probably smiled at these words, aware that intellec-
tually she could never match her Alexander but that she
brought to him other and more important gifts. As a great
philosopher has remarked, "the heart hath reasons that the
reason knows nothing of." As a loyal and sympathetic companion (who, far from tolerating her husband's faults, was
simply blissfully oblivious to them), as a selflessly devoted
mother of what would be a family of eight children, Betsey
Schuyler Hamilton was way and above the best thing that
ever happened to the mental genius she married.

Genius alone would never have carried Hamilton to the
heights of statesmanship. Even as a swaggering aide-de-camp
he was more than a bright young man. His mind was too
broad, his vision too wide, his sense of moral responsibility
too strong for him ever to regard any of his tasks at headquarters as an end in itself. He saw even the smallest of them in a

larger context, in relation, that is, to the problems confronting his adopted nation. Constantly he projected his thinking forward. Like Washington, like many of the great men of his country's heroic age, he realized that for the American people, winning the war would only be the first—and easiest —step toward the accomplishment of that most difficult of cooperative enterprises, the creation of an adequate system of government.

Fortunately for Hamilton's development, and his country's too, he had learned early in life that clues to the solution of problems are available in books. Busy as he was at headquarters, he read voluminously. It is impossible to trace his leading ideas to any one author or group of authors. The way he evolved them brings to mind a statement of the seventeenth-century French playwright who called himself Molière. Accused of stealing his plots from the comedy writers of ancient Rome, Molière indulged in a Gallic shrug. "I take my own," he said, "where I find it."

Hamilton arrived at his concept of good government, his political creed, in the same way. Early in the war he read the classics with which every well-educated eighteenth-century man was familiar. Later, along about 1778, his reading began to reflect an increasing interest in public finance. He turned to the writings of such European economists as Malachy Postlethwayt and David Hume. He took some notions from each of these and other thinkers, considered them in the light of his country's difficulties, altered them accordingly, and fused them together. The result, his personal philosophy, was neither "Postlethwaytism" nor "Humeism" nor "anybody-elseism." It was what people would later call Hamiltonianism.

During the winter of 1779–80, he began to put his mature

views into writing. First in several long letters to men in high places, then in published essays, he set forth the major elements of Hamiltonianism. One of his firmest convictions was that the country must have strong central government, with the states taking secondary roles. Books alone had not guided him to this position. At one time practically every one of his friends had viewed his own state—his "country," as Jefferson often spoke of Virginia—as meriting the first claim on his loyalties. An immigrant from the West Indies, Hamilton had no state. With no provincial loyalties to unlearn, he was a born nationalist.

He was also a born aristocrat, the grandson of a Scottish lord and all the more insistent on being so regarded because of the irregularity of his birth. This fact had much to do with his assertion that the national government should be directed, not by the common people but by the upper classes —by "the rich, the wise and the good," to use a phrase mouthed with some frequency by the conservatives of his era.

Hamilton had not always thought along these lines. "I believe," he wrote in 1777, "that the perils some purport to see in majority rule are exaggerated." A year later he was backing away from this democratic stance with the alacrity of a man removing himself from the path of a wild beast.

By this time, in point of fact, he had concluded that the "majority"—people in the mass—*were* a wild beast. Here again his principal teacher was not books but personal observation. His distrust of people arose from two sources. One was his memory of the human perfidy he had witnessed as a mercantile clerk in the West Indies. The other was his experience while serving at Washington's headquarters. During the terrible winter at Valley Forge and the even crueler one two years later at Morristown, he saw men starve and die because other men sold their grain and cattle to private individuals able to pay more than the government could. Bitter outbursts at the wickedness of mankind run through his correspondence: "Experience," he wote in 1783, "is a continual comment on the worthlessness of the human race. I know few men estimable, fewer amiable."

At the heart of his political creed was the notion that the government should pursue policies attractive to the wealthy. Hamilton, let it be repeated, did not exempt rich people from his statement that few men were "estimable, fewer amiable." On the contrary he found the rich more susceptible than most groups to the siren songs of greed and self-interest. His point was that no government could endure without their help. He assumed that if the government supported them, they would support it. Hence his contention that a government's first duty was to protect the right of citizens to the peaceful enjoyment of their property. When critics accused him of putting property rights before human rights, he answered that the two were interdependent. "When property is insecure," he argued, "men are not free." He did not consider all property rights as equally sacred. He recommended abolition of those "contrary to the social order and the permanent welfare of society." In his purview the horrible example of this "wrong kind of property right" was slavery.

In several of the early expressions of his philosophy, he dwelt on the unhappy financial condition of the country. Without taxing powers and desperate for funds to run the war, Congress had turned to the printing press. Since the opening of the conflict, it had issued vast amounts of paper money. As this had nothing behind it but Congress' promise to pay, the inevitable effects had ensued: depreciation and inflation. Continental currency had fallen swiftly; prices had as swiftly risen. By 1779 a continental dollar was worth only one-fortieth of its face value. Much of the misery at Valley Forge and Morristown originated in the inability of the government, under these circumstances, to purchase what the army needed.

In a letter to Robert Morris, the brilliant Philadelphia merchant and statesman later known as "the financier of the Revolution," Hamilton offered remedies for this situation. One of his suggestions showed a nice understanding of mass psychology. He pointed out to Morris that although Great Britain might be wicked, her money—the English pound— was good. On the other hand, America might be virtuous, but her dollar was bad. He suggested, therefore, that the Philadelphia merchant use his influence to persuade Congress to stop issuing paper dollars and to issue paper pounds instead. "It will produce a useful illusion," he wrote. "Mankind are much led by sounds and appearances; and the currency having changed its name will seem to have changed its nature."

He realized that the good effects of this measure would be shortlived at best. As a permanent remedy he advocated establishment of a national bank. He proposed that Congress put up part of the bank's funds, and that private individuals subscribe the balance. One of the bank's duties and privileges would be to issue paper money. Hamilton reasoned that since this paper would be backed by the resources of both the bank and the government, it would circulate at or near face value. An inventive proposal, this. Eighteenth-century Europe had a number of banks, including the Bank of England, a national institution somewhat similar to the one Hamilton outlined in his letter to Robert Morris; but prior to 1781 America had no banks of any sort. Characteristically, Hamilton was ahead of his times. His national bank would have to wait until years later when, as the first Secretary of the Treasury under the Constitution, he would make it a part of his grand scheme to put America's newly born Federal government on the path to financial stability.

During the period of Hamilton's courtship and marriage, the war moved into what was to be its final chapter. In the summer of 1780, France sent another fleet along with more than five thousand fighting men under Jean Baptiste de Vimeur, Count de Rochambeau. Hamilton was a member of Washington's party when in September the American commander journeyed from an encampment at New Bridge, New Jersey, to Hartford, Connecticut, to meet with the French general. It was on their return trip from this council of war, during a stop on the eastern shore of the Hudson, that Washington and his aides learned of Benedict Arnold's treason. Their discovery came in time to prevent Arnold from delivering West Point to the enemy, too late to prevent the traitor himself from escaping to the safety of a British warship in the Hudson.

Involved with Arnold was the handsome young British officer, Major John André, whose capture shortly before the traitor's flight had brought the conspiracy to light. André was an appealing young man, bright, gracious, brave. Hamilton watched with approval his dignified behavior before the military court that condemned him to die on the gallows as a spy. He could not object to the court's verdict, for André had been caught in civilian clothes behind the American lines, an action carrying the death penalty under the rules of war. It was another story, however, when the gallant English officer requested a favor that in Hamilton's opinion should have been granted. André asked permission to die before a firing squad rather than at the end of a hangman's rope. When Washington said no to this petition, Hamilton's always simmering disapproval of his chief swelled into contempt. "Some people," he scoffed, "are only sensible to motives of policy, and sometimes, from a narrow disposition, mistake it."

He had never been content at his secretary's desk. After André's execution in October his restlessness grew. Frequently in the past he had confided to friends his desire to hear again "the charming sound of bullets." A contradictory young man was Colonel Hamilton: old far beyond his years when he took up his pen to instruct the most important men of his country on the principles of finance and government; young as the boy who years before had written "I wish there was a war!" when the opportunity arose to indulge his craving for military renown. The arrival of Rochambeau and his division, the rumors of more French aid in the offing—these indications that the war could not last much longer created in him a raging determination to take to the battlefield and seek his moment of glory before it was too late.

Twice he had asked Washington for a field command, twice he had been turned down. In the fall of 1780, influential friends tried to obtain for him a post that would permit him to spend at least part of his time in the field. By the time Washington had established winter quarters in New Windsor, New York, however, it was clear nothing was to come of these efforts.

Washington, at this period, was under a strain himself. In

the South things were going badly for the American cause. In the North there were recurrent mutinies, the rebellion of unpaid, ill-housed, ill-fed, and, in some cases, literally unclothed soldiers. Pending additional aid from France, the American military leader was marking time, meanwhile pondering whether he and Rochambeau should plan an attack on Sir Henry Clinton at New York or a move south in an effort to halt the British advance below the Potomac. To this atmosphere of uncertainty and stress, add Hamilton's resentment at Washington's treatment of Major André, and it is easy to see why on February 17, 1781, their always edgy relationship suddenly and emotionally snapped.

The incident that separated them was small but revealing. That morning the two men chanced to pass each other on the stair of the headquarters house at New Windsor. Washington, en route to his second-floor room, asked Hamilton to join him there. Hamilton said he would as soon as he had delivered a letter "of a pressing nature" to a fellow staff-member on the floor below.

This errand completed, he was hastening to keep his appointment when the Marquis de Lafayette accosted him in the first-floor hall, detaining him briefly "on a matter of business." Breaking off their conversation as soon as courtesy permitted, Hamilton moved on, only to discover as he mounted the stair that the commander-in-chief was not in his room. He was standing on the landing above, glowering down.

He said, "Colonel Hamilton, you have kept me waiting . . . these ten minutes. I must tell you, sir, you treat me with disrespect."

Hamilton replied, "I am not conscious of it, sir, but since you have thought it necessary to tell me so, we part."

Then Washington said, "Very well, sir, if it be your choice."

An hour later Washington sent a messenger to Hamilton to suggest that the two of them meet for "a candid conversation, to heal a difference which could not have happened but in a moment of passion." To this generous near-apology, Hamilton replied with a message so lengthy and so meticulously organized as to suggest that he had long been looking for a pretext to resign. He begged to be excused from an interview certain to be mutually painful. His decision to leave his post was irrevocable, but he would remain until Washington could find a suitable replacement for him. He remained about six weeks. Then he and Betsey moved to a rented house at DePeyster's Point, across the Hudson River from New Windsor.

In this impetuous (one is tempted to say childish) manner, Hamilton terminated his services as aide-de-camp to Washington. In a long letter to his father-in-law, he recorded his own version of how the breach had occurred. He assured Schuyler that he had not kept his chief waiting for ten minutes, as Washington had claimed; only "two minutes" at the most. He revealed that he had "always disliked the office as an aide-de-camp as having in it a kind of personal dependence." He had accepted the invitation to join Washington's staff only because friends had painted the general's character in rosy hues. Experience had taught him that their praise was "unfounded." It had not taken him long, he wrote, to discover that Washington "was neither remarkable for delicacy nor good temper."

If by this self-justifying letter, Hamilton hoped to win his father-in-law's approval of what he had done, he was disappointed. The patroon admired Washington as much as he admired Hamilton. He hinted that it would have been manly of the younger officer to have taken the older one's many worries into consideration and to have closed the incident on the stair with an apology for keeping the commander-in-chief waiting. He expressed the fear that it was unwise of Hamilton to give up the useful work he could do at headquarters for the transient éclat of martial adventure. The wisdom and restraint age brings to some were reflected in Schuyler's observation that it "falls to the lot of few men to pass through life without one of those unguarded moments which wound the feelings of a friend."

The tone of the patroon's letter was warm but sad, as though for the first time he realized that there was a strain of recklessness in his brilliant son-in-law, that once Alexander Hamilton made up his mind to do something, even something detrimental to himself, no one could stop him.

☆   ☆   ☆

In the letter to his father-in-law, Hamilton had predicted that Washington would hold a grudge against him. This assumption rested on a misreading of the Virginian's character. A few months later the commander-in-chief presented him with the opportunity to do and dare he so longed for—the command of a newly formed battalion.

By this date, July 31, 1781, the military situation had altered drastically. Charles Lord Cornwallis, leader of the British forces in the South, had stationed himself at Yorktown, far out on one of the Virginia peninsulas that prod the waters of Chesapeake Bay. A French fleet sailing up from the West Indies had Cornwallis blocked off on the bay side; and when in August, Washington, Rochambeau, and their allied armies marched south to attack the trapped British general on the land side, Hamilton and his battalion marched with them.

During the siege of Yorktown, the new battalion commander squeezed every possible ounce of glory from the situation. He was not alone in this. A certain derring-do characterized the behavior of the Americans generally. It arose from their annoyance at the British regulars' frequently avowed contempt for "rebellious peasants," buttressed by the "peasants' " low opinion of British marksmanship. One militiaman placed himself on a parapet in full view of the enemy. There, according to a diary-keeper, he "d———d his soul if he would dodge the buggers—and brandished his spade at every ball that was fired till, unfortunately, a ball came and put an end to his caper."

Unwilling to be outdone by a militiaman, Hamilton ordered his troops to mount the same parapet and go through the manual of arms. British shot had been coming thick and fast, but, dumbfounded at this display of foolhardiness, the enemy gunners held their fire until the exercises ended.

When the time came for the big American-French assault on Cornwallis' works, the honor of leading the American half of the charge fell to a colonel attached to Lafayette's headquarters. Happily for Hamilton, the attack was scheduled for a day on which he had been named officer of the day. Making the most of this circumstance, he persuaded Washington that he, rather than Lafayette's aide, should have command of the assaulting party.

So it was that on the night of October 14, Hamilton and his troops overran and captured a strategic British redoubt. In the fierce fighting, seven men and officers were killed, fifteen wounded. Hamilton survived unscathed. The action lasted only ten minutes, but to the one-time aide-de-camp they were probably the most satisfactory minutes of his life.

On the following day Cornwallis hoisted the white flag, and two days later the ceremonies of surrender took place. Except for some minor engagements in the South, the Revolutionary War was over.

Hamilton hastened home to his Betsey. During the idle interval following his resignation from headquarters, he had begun the study of law. Eager to get back to his textbooks, he realized that "to avoid inferiority" in his chosen profession, he "must be laborious." Then too, his wife was expecting their first child, a boy who, born on January 22, 1782, would receive the name Philip, in honor of his prideful grandfather.

6

Nation-Builder

Home from the wars and in Albany, Hamilton studied in the law office of Colonel Robert Troup, his former college roommate, and helped Betsey care for their little son. "You cannot imagine," he wrote a friend, "how entirely domestic I am growing. I lose all my taste for the pursuit of ambition. I sigh for nothing but the company of my wife and baby."

A more inaccurate picture of Alexander Hamilton would be hard to conceive. The pursuits of ambition would seldom if ever lose their fascination for him, and he had given too much thought to the fate of his country to be indifferent to it now. As he made doting-father sounds over Philip's cradle or paced Colonel Troup's office, a copy of Blackstone or of Coke in hand, he brooded on the problems that the coming of peace had dumped upon the American people.

Complex as these problems were, nearly all of them stemmed from the nature of the national government that the Articles of Confederation, as adopted by Congress in 1777 and ratified by the states four years later, had only recently breathed into existence. A flickering existence, for as Hamilton had recognized for years, the Confederation was not of the stuff that endures. Its feebleness was an outgrowth of the very spirit that had produced the war. A people who in 1775 had rebelled against strong central government in England could hardly be expected only a few years later to take kindly to the same kind of government on their own soil. They much preferred to leave the bulk of their country's political power where it already resided—in their respective states.

Under the Articles of Confederation the national government consisted of a one-house legislature, a continuation of the Continental Congress officially known as The United States in Congress Assembled. The powers that the Articles imparted to the United States in Congress Assembled were infinitesimal compared with those that they specifically withheld. Congress could not lay or collect taxes. It could not regulate commerce among the states.

What could it do? It could issue and borrow money. It could raise armies and declare wars. It could appoint such forerunners of today's Cabinet officers as the Superintendent of Finance and the Secretary of Foreign Affairs. It could deal with foreign governments and negotiate treaties, although this power, like most of its powers, was mightier in theory than in fact since no treaties or alliances could be effected without the consent of the majority of the states. To run the government and pay off a giant war debt, it could request the states to levy and gather what were called continental taxes and turn these over to Congress. Unfortunately the Articles did not compel the states to do this. Consequently, what Congress got depended on what the states wanted to give. From his elevated but impecunious position as Superintendent of Finance, genial Robert Morris of Philadelphia quipped that the Articles of Confederation secured to Congress "the privilege of asking everything" and to the states "the prerogative of granting nothing."

The amazing thing about this bird called on to fly without wings was not that it eventually fell; that was inevitable. The amazing thing was that during its short life it achieved some sensational flights. At war's end it negotiated a treaty of peace that has been called "the greatest triumph in the history of American diplomacy," so generous were its terms from the viewpoint of the new republic. Even as its death warrant was being written at the constitutional convention in Philadelphia, the old Congress of the Confederation brought forth the Ordinance of 1787, one of the most important steps in the development of the American nation. Popularly known as the Northwest Ordinance, this document organized the huge western territory running north of the Ohio River from the Appalachians to the Mississippi. It set up the machinery which later enabled the country to expand in an orderly and peaceful manner from thirteen little states hemmed between sea and mountains to fifty states, extending from the Atlantic to the western beaches of Hawaii far out in the Pacific, from Florida on the south to Alaska in the shadow of the North Pole.

Most important of all, the Confederation provided the leaders of the new republic with a school of nation-building. When the Founding Fathers met in Philadelphia to form "a more perfect Union," the Constitution they wrote was in many respects simply the Articles of Confederation turned inside out. Their experience under the Articles had taught them a valuable lesson, namely, what not to do.

In 1782 this "school of nation-building" had few more attentive pupils than Alexander Hamilton. Viewing from Albany the plight of his country, he could only conclude that he was gazing on "an awful spectacle." When the opportunity came to return to public life, he jumped at the chance, apprehending that the only way he could influence events was to be in the thick of them. The letter he had written to Robert Morris, prescribing ways out of America's financial labyrinth, had not gone unnoticed. Before Hamilton could complete his studies and be admitted to the bar—a three-year undertaking that he accomplished in five months—he was in receipt of an offer from Morris to serve as Receiver of the Continental Taxes for the State of New York.

In view of his state's reluctance to raise money for the national government, the job was not a particularly gratifying one. Still he was happy to have it. It placed him again on that brightly lighted stage of public affairs, away from which he was never wholly himself. In 1782 Congress called on New York for eight million dollars. Hamilton, after three months of back-breaking labor, had collected about five per cent of this amount when in July the state legislature rescued him from the frustrations of a thankless job by sending him to Philadelphia as a delegate to the Continental Congress.

To Hamilton the national legislature, for all its limitations, was an ideal platform from which to put forth his political doctrines. With a wife and infant son to support, however, he could ill afford to devote himself exclusively to the public weal. Abandoning his seat in July of 1783, he returned to Albany long enough to compose a political tract and to make preparations for moving to New York City. There he established his home and his office at 57 Wall Street, and within a few months had become one of the most sought after members of a new crop of young lawyers that included such dazzling courtroom performers as Brockholst Livingston, Edward Livingston, and Aaron Burr.

His practice was mostly civil disputes, with now and then a criminal case, as when he defended one Murphy, accused of attacking Margaret Russell "with force and arms to wit with Sword and Stones and Knives. . . ." In postwar America feeling was rife against loyalists, those citizens who had sided with the enemy. This sentiment was especially strong in New York City, only recently evacuated by its long-time British occupiers. In court and out, with a fearless indifference to popular prejudice that would characterize his entire career, Hamilton defended the local loyalists against hastily passed state laws aimed at depriving them of their civic rights and property.

It appalled him to see thousands of them fleeing to Canada or England, driven into exile by what to him were vengeful and discriminatory laws. Among those leaving the state were men of proven ability and enterprise. Their departure, in his opinion, deprived the country of some of the talents it needed to help solve the awesome problems of nation-building.

Those problems were never far from the center of his consciousness. His practice was heavy, his family was growing— a second child, a daughter, in 1783; a third, another son, in 1786—but somehow he found time, as in the past, to put his opinions in print. Newspaper articles and pamphlets flowed from his pen. He was a gifted and astoundingly speedy writer. There was a clarity about his essays, an engaging lightness that conveyed even his most profound thoughts as readily to the man in the street as to the learned and the scholarly. It is another sidelight on the duality of his make-up that he, the aristocrat, went to such pains to woo the understanding and support of the hoi polloi he professed to disdain.

The theme of his major tracts at this point was the need for a more vigorous national government. Casting his eyes over the domestic scene, he sounded an ominous warning. Congress must receive the power to regulate commerce among the states. Otherwise, left to their own devices in this regard, the states would soon be warring on each other. Then the cause for which so many men had died on the battlefields of the Revolution, the creation of "a great Federal Republic, closely linked in the pursuit of a common interest," would be lost forever.

He did not have to look far for object lessons in support of his fears. Some of the states were already at each other's throats. The citizens of Connecticut and New Jersey were complaining bitterly at paying to New York State duties on foreign-made goods reaching them through the port of New York City. In 1782 a Connecticut-born schoolmaster-lawyer named Noah Webster was going back and forth on the face of the land, saying precisely what Hamilton was saying: the union could not survive without a more effective general government. Young Webster's one-man crusade rested on the strongest of motives: his personal interests. He had not yet produced his monumental dictionary, but he had published the first of the little spelling books that during the next half-century Americans would purchase to the extent of sixty million copies. His first speller was selling well, but he was making little money on it because Congress lacked the power to issue a copyright law. Thus any unscrupulous person could publish the book without paying royalties to the author. Webster wanted a national government strong enough to insure him the just rewards of his labors.

Turning to the international scene, Hamilton found even more cogent arguments for his position. Directly or indirectly, the income of most Americans came from trade with other countries. Diligently Congress undertook to make treaties of commerce with the nations of Europe. Even when these efforts succeeded, little good ensued. Congress had the power to make the treaties, but it could not enforce them. There was nothing in the Articles of Confederation to stop individual states from nullifying a trade agreement by ignoring or violating its provisions.

Prior to the war thousands of Americans had depended for their livelihoods on a flourishing trade with Great Britain and her possessions in the West Indies. As colonials the American people had conducted this trade under generally favorable conditions. As citizens of an independent nation they now found themselves facing a host of crippling restrictions.

England imposed heavy duties on American imports. She flooded the largely unprotected American market with low-priced English goods. To a significant extent she limited her purchase of American goods to those carried on English ships. These policies of mercantilism, as they were called, bore hard on American merchants, tradesmen, ship-owners and ship-builders. Before the war, for example, the whaling industry of Massachusetts had brought to the mariners of that province more than eight hundred thousand dollars a year. After the war this source of revenue all but dried up when England placed a duty of ninety cents a ton on American whale oil.

Efforts by the individual states to get better terms from England by taxing her imports were unavailing. For one thing, the states passed different and often conflicting tariff laws. For another, some of them refused to pass any. The citizens of the five southern states were not interested in discouraging the influx of cheap British goods. They made their living by exporting their staple crops to Europe. They had no infant industries to protect. Nor did they much care whether their duty-free tobacco crossed the Atlantic on English or on American bottoms.

Only a commercial treaty with England could resolve these problems. But England was not about to enter into such an arrangement with a Congress that not only was unable to pay the interest on its war debt but, during most years, was unable to induce the states to send it enough money to pay its daily expenses.

England's disrespect for the Confederation expressed itself in other ways. Contrary to the terms of the peace treaty, she continued to enjoy a fur monopoly in the American West by holding on to a string of military outposts in that region. Citizens living on the frontier complained to Congress, and Congress complained to London. There the matter ended. Complaints of this sort to a foreign government were meaningless in the absence of an army to back them up; and an army was one of the many luxuries the weak American government could not afford. Almost the minute the peace treaty was signed Congress had dismissed all of the Continental Army save the small force needed to guard the stores at West Point and elsewhere. Since Congress still owed a good deal of money to the soldiers of the old army, raising a new one was out of the question.

During the five uneasy years following the signing of the peace treaty in 1783, the factor that did more than any other to create a desire for a stronger central government was this inability of the Confederation to compel England to relinquish the western forts and to modify her restrictions on American trade.

Hamilton placed his pen and his voice behind repeated attempts to strengthen the government by amending the Articles. When one by one these projects collapsed, however, he was not unduly distressed. He preferred a weak national authority to none at all; but he was certain, and had been for years, that in the long pull the Confederation, however altered, would not work. His personal prescription for America's ills was a more drastic one. He wanted to see the present government scrapped, and a better one put in its place; and when in 1786 the opportunity arose to inaugurate a movement to this end, he acted quickly and boldly.

Early that year, Virginia, egged on by James Madison, invited the other states to a convention at Annapolis, Maryland, to consider the commercial woes of the country and to draft recommendations for alleviating them. Hamilton had only recently been elected to the New York legislature. Although his term there had not yet begun, he persuaded that body to send him to Annapolis as one of his state's delegates.

Of the thirteen states, only five were represented at Annapolis—New York, Virginia, Pennsylvania, New Jersey, and Delaware. Some of the other states named delegates, but neglected to send them. Maryland, whose capital city was host to the convention in September of 1786, did not even bother to name any. On the surface, the convention was a failure—but in its very weakness Hamilton spied a glittering opportunity. The incomplete records show that it was chiefly his quick and audacious thinking that converted this tiny gathering into a stepping-stone to the larger gathering that a few months later would produce the Federal Constitution.

It would be misleading to suggest that Hamilton brought off this master-stroke singlehandedly. Madison of Virginia and some of the other delegates had much to do with it. The fact remains that Hamilton's was the principal guiding hand. It was he who most persuasively pointed out that it would be futile for five states to recommend a system for governing the commerce of thirteen states. Rather than attempt the impossible, he proposed that the convention issue a report summoning all of the states "to meet at Philadelphia on the second Monday of next May" to adopt measures for regulating interstate commerce, along with "such further provisions as should appear necessary to render the constitution [the Articles] adequate to the exigencies of the Union. . . ."

To this procedure the other delegates unanimously agreed. As a result, the only action of the Annapolis convention was the issuance of a document that for sheer shrewdness of language has few equals in history. It did not so much as use the words "constitutional convention"; but in recommending that the states empower their delegates to the Philadelphia meeting to consider *political* as well as commercial problems, the report become in fact a bid to just such a convention.

Attempts to bring about a national meeting for the purpose of writing a new Constitution had been tried before. All had failed. This one too might have come to nothing had it not been for an event that was getting underway even as the delegates to the Annapolis convention finished their business and started home. Up in western Massachusetts, the state militia were coping with an outbreak of civil disobedience subsequently known as Shays' Rebellion. This unsuccessful attempt by impoverished farmers to close the courts, and thus rid themselves of a crushing burden of debt, frightened conservative Americans. Many discerned in the revolt the possibility that without a stronger national government all debts, public and private, would soon be annihilated and all commercial contracts reduced to scraps of paper. By May of 1787, when the representatives of twelve of the thirteen states gathered in Philadelphia for the Federal convention, the sentiment for stronger government had reached such a pitch that the man chosen to preside, George Washington, had no sooner lowered his gavel for the first time than delegates were on their feet clamoring for an end to the Confederation and its replacement by a more energetic system.

The New York legislature named three delegates to the convention. Hamilton was one of them but, because of the political situation in his state, his direct influence on the deliberations at Philadelphia was small. New York's affairs were dominated by its shrewd and able governor, George Clinton, and his loyal followers, the "Clintonians." Strong national government was anathema to the governor. "His Excellency's" dislike of it rested on something more immediate than his reiterated fear that the "super-state" Hamilton wanted would rob the American people of their liberties. Of all the states, New York probably benefited most from things as they were. Under the Articles of Confederation, Congress could not levy a tariff on foreign imports. But the states could, and New York did, deriving from the duties collected at her busy harbor enough money to pay the bulk of the state's expenses. For His Excellency this was pleasant. It was also pleasant for His Excellency's lightly taxed subjects, who had already shown their gratitude by electing him to the governorship four times running and were about to hand him three more terms.

Both of Hamilton's fellow delegates to the Federal convention were Clintonians, determined to oppose any attempt to abolish the Confederation. At Philadelphia each state could cast only one vote, a rule that made Hamilton an ineffectual minority of one in his own delegation.

His inability to make his vote count did not stop him from using his voice. When on June 18 he rose from his seat in the handsome meeting room at the eastern end of what is now Independence Hall, it was to make the longest speech of the convention.

By this time the outline of America's future government had begun to emerge from the debates. Many details remained to be thrashed out, but it was clear that the Federal Constitution would provide for a three-branch government consisting of a one-man executive to be known as the President, a two-house Congress, and a judiciary system surmounted by the Supreme Court.

Hamilton expressed no objections to this framework. He merely offered "certain propositions" concerning it. He proposed that the people of the country determine the membership of the House of Representatives by direct vote. His theory was that a House chosen in this manner would give Americans a legal outlet, a vent, for their "democratic impulses."

But as Hamilton had said before, and would often repeat, he was afraid of "democratic licentiousness." He was convinced that, unless subjected to "adequate safeguards," democracy would eventually degenerate into anarchy and violence. To guard against this outcome, he proposed "checking" the democratic House of Representatives with an "aristocratic Senate" and a "monarchial presidency." To this end he suggested that both President and Senators be chosen by an electoral college. He further proposed that once chosen they remain in office "during good behavior," which was to say for life. He argued that under this arrangement—this "high-toned government," as he called it—Americans could enjoy the benefits of democracy without stumbling into its pitfalls.

The constitution-makers met behind closed doors, but the seal of secrecy under which they worked did not extend to their memories. In the years ahead, some of them, recalling Hamilton's plea for a "monarchial presidency" on that hot afternoon in 1787, would accuse him of wanting to put a king over the American people. In truth this charge was not a description but a caricature of his views. "I am affectionately attached to the republican theory," he asserted. "I desire above all things to see the equality of political rights, exclusive of hereditary distinction, firmly established by practical demonstration of its being consistent with the order and happiness of society." What Hamilton advocated was not a monarchy but a government so balanced that no group of people could dominate any other group. "Give all power to the many," he would write later, and "they will oppress the few. Give all power to the few, they will oppress the many. Both therefore ought to have power, that each may defend itself against the other."

No doubt Hamilton would have been less frank on that afternoon in Philadelphia had he thought that his listeners would act on his ideas. He knew there was little chance of that. He was asking for a government stronger than the most nationalistic members of the convention were known to favor. "Our situation," he told the delegates, "is peculiar—*it leaves room to dream. . . .*" With these words he signaled that his purpose in speaking was not to produce action but thought. Before putting their ideas into final form, while they still had *room to dream*, he wanted the Founding Fathers to consider every conceivable form that a government suitable to America might take.

When in September the delegates completed their work, the plan of government they asked the thirteen states to approve bore little resemblance to Hamilton's "high-toned" system. Even so, he promptly announced his intention of supporting it with all the talents at his disposal. This was not the act of an opportunist. It was the decision of a statesman, convinced that with all its weaknesses the document written at Philadelphia was too much of an improvement on the Articles of Confederation to be passed over. Had this "spirit of accommodation," as Washington called it, permeated the rest of Alexander Hamilton's life, his career might have run a less violent course. Never again would the political Hotspur of his era so completely subjugate his personal preferences to what in his view was his country's wellbeing.

With the adjournment of the Federal convention, the struggle for better government shifted from Philadelphia to the country as a whole. One by one, the legislatures set up machinery for electing delegates to the state conventions that would decide the issue by ratifying or rejecting the proposed Constitution. New political terms sprang into prominence. People spoke of those who approved of what the Founding Fathers had done as "Federalists," of those who did not as "Antifederalists."

The battle was a fierce one. In a letter to a friend, Virginia's brilliant little statesman, James Madison, observed that the "newspapers . . . team with controversial publications."

"Team" they did. Especially in New York where Governor Clinton launched the Antifederalists' campaign with a series of newspaper articles castigating the document framed at Philadelphia as a blueprint for a "vile and arbitrary aristocracy." Federalist Hamilton's first action was to dash off a series of answers to Clinton's arguments. His second was to induce Madison and John Jay to collaborate with him in writing *The Federalist*, a collection of articles, eighty-five in all, analyzing the principles underlying nearly every phrase, clause, and sentence in the proposed Constitution.

Each of the authors of this most famous political commentary in American history used the same pen name, "Publius." Because of ill health, Jay withdrew from the undertaking after contributing five papers to the collection. Hamilton and Madison pushed on. Working fast, often turning out as many as four articles a week, they completed their ambitious project in seven months. A New York newspaper published the first Federalist Paper on October 29, 1787, the last one on August 16 of the following year.

Both Hamilton and Madison had to perform their literary chores during days crowded with private affairs. Hamilton penned many of his Federalist Papers while traveling the New York court circuit, as all lawyers did in his era; from one court to another in his state. We have a dramatic picture of him composing the introductory essay by the tossing light of an oil lamp in the cabin of a Hudson River sloop. Although some dispute still exists over who wrote which of the Federalist Papers, it appears that Hamilton did fifty-four of them, Madison twenty-six.

The authors of the essays did not confine themselves to defending the Constitution. Their every word portrayed a mutual desire to be political scientists first, and propagandists only incidentally. Neither man went out of his way to flatter his readers. Both agreed, in Madison's words, that "if men were angels" there would be no need to set up a government of any sort. Hamilton made no pretense of being satisfied with the Constitution as it stood, frankly avowing his disappointment that the Founding Fathers had not seen fit to devise a system closer to his own autocratic ideas. Madison, in his famous Federalist Paper Number Ten, made it perfectly clear to those who bothered to read him closely that the framers of the Constitution were not a bevy of idealists, solely concerned with abstract justice. He admitted that to some degree the document they had written reflected their economic interests. Hamilton, in Paper Number Seventy-eight, erected the foundation of what has been called "the most original construction in American jurisprudence," the doctrine of judicial review—the principle that the courts may nullify the laws of Congress by declaring them unconstitutional.

The long-range effects of the Federalist Papers were to be extensive, but the immediate ones were modest. For generations men and women around the world would turn to these tracts for a better understanding of the American experiment in free government; but there are no indications that in its own day *The Federalist* exerted a substantial influence on events.

The same can be said of the literary efforts of such leading Antifederalists as Clinton of New York, Elbridge Gerry of Massachusetts, and George Mason of Virginia. The swiftness with which American citizens voted for the Constitution

suggests that most of them had made up their minds before
their leaders could get around to telling them what to think.

The final article of the Constitution stipulated that it was
to take effect when ratified by nine of the thirteen states.
Three states had ratified the charter by the end of 1787; a
total of eight had done so when in June of 1788 the delegates to the New York ratifying convention began gathering
in the little Hudson River town of Poughkeepsie. There
during the next few weeks Alexander Hamilton was to perform the most astounding political feat of his career.

Standing among the Hudson River highlands "92 chains
and 70 links due east of the river," Poughkeepsie in the
summer of 1788 had almost a thousand inhabitants, was the
capital of prosperous Dutchess County, had been the capital
of the state off and on since 1777, and enjoyed the benefits of
a lively shipbuilding industry. Neat drainage ditches lined
its main thoroughfares. The stone courthouse—meeting
place of the convention at the juncture of Main Street and
the Post Road leading north from New York City to Albany
—had a Palladian window above its arched entranceway,
eight ordinary windows across the first floor front, nine
across the second, and a handsome open cupola.

As the members of the convention began to arrive, a
young Poughkeepsie lawyer named James Kent, later to become one of the legal lights of the English-speaking world,
found it easy to distinguish the Antifederalist followers of
Governor Clinton from their Federalist opponents. The
"Antis," as Kent called them, were jubilant. In a statewide
popular election, they had triumphed in every section of the
state except New York City and the counties immediately

adjoining it. Of the sixty-five men named to the convention, only nineteen were in favor of ratification. "How are the mighty fallen!" a leading Anti exulted in a pointed reference to the claim of the Federalists that they represented the interests of the "well-born."

Fallen the New York Federalists were, but their leader, Alexander Hamilton, had not come to Poughkeepsie as one of his city's delegates to pronounce a funeral oration over the work of the Founding Fathers. Overwhelming as the opposition was, he was not without hope. He was aware of many shades of opinion among the Antis. Some were totally opposed to the Constitution. Others stood ready to approve it "conditionally"—with the proviso, that is, that certain amendments be added to it. He was also aware that, since eight states in a row had endorsed the Constitution, many of the New York Antis were reluctant about putting their state in the position of being the first to turn it down.

It so happened, too, that conventions called to consider the Constitution were in process elsewhere, notably in Virginia and New Hampshire. This being the case, the strategy of the New York Antis, as their own convention began in Poughkeepsie on June 17, was to prevent any final action until these states were heard from.

To Hamilton this policy of delay presented obvious advantages. It gave him time to marshal his outnumbered forces and to put the case for the Constitution before the assemblage in the hope that some of the more moderate Antis would change their minds. The skill with which he carried on these maneuvers during the opening sessions prompted one observer to liken the situation to a "Homeric battle, Hamilton against a host."

As the days moved on, in truth, the battle came close to

being Hamilton of New York City against Melancton Smith of Dutchess County. At the initial session the delegates elected Governor Clinton president of the convention, but in the ensuing debates forty-four-year-old Smith rapidly emerged as the real leader of the Antis.

Smith was a thoughtful, reasonable, and deeply learned man who, born of poor and obscure parents, had by his own efforts become a successful lawyer and merchant. Young James Kent of Poughkeepsie, closely watching the thrust and parry of a stimulating forensic duel, was delighted to see the great Alexander Hamilton pitted against so worthy an opponent. In Kent's opinion there "was no person to be compared" with Smith in "his powers of acute and logical discussion." His style of speaking "was dry, plain and syllogistic, and it behooved his adversary to examine well the ground on which they started" lest he find himself trapped in the "subtle web" of the Dutchess merchant-attorney's reasoning.

For three weeks the clash continued with neither side drawing blood. Then, like increasingly more disturbing earthquakes, came a succession of crises.

On June 24 word arrived that New Hampshire had ratified. To the more moderate Antis this was jolting news. It meant that legally, if not yet in fact, the Confederation was no more. If New York refused to ratify now, it would soon find itself living outside of the Federal union that the endorsement of the Constitution by nine of the states had created. But Hamilton's hopes that New Hampshire's action would diminish the ranks of the opposition were shortlived. In his quiet, unhurried way, Melancton Smith rallied his faltering forces—and the argument went on.

In the early afternoon of July 2, Governor Clinton de-

serted the presiding officer's chair to deliver one of his rare
speeches. The other delegates were listening to him with the
respect due the chief magistrate of their state when, in the
words of a diary-keeping witness, "such a buzz" went
through the meeting room "that little of His Excellency's
speech was heard." On the dirt street out front, a rider had
dismounted from a hard-ridden bay horse. He brought a
packet of dispatches for Hamilton. Among them was the no-
tification that under the ingenious generalship of James
Madison the Federalists had won in Richmond. State number ten, Virginia, had ratified the Constitution.

Federalist citizens of the little town, drawn to the courthouse by the excitement, heard the news, promptly produced a fife and drum corps from somewhere, and began
marching around the building. In the meeting hall there
was an upsurge of emotions that off and on for the next two
days disrupted the proceedings.

Virginia was the wealthiest and the most populous of all
the states. Moderate Antis who had bent a little at the
thought of New York living outside of the union with Virginia also on the outside showed signs of breaking at the
prospect of being on the outside with powerful Virginia in.

But again Hamilton's prayer that a development in another state would turn the tide went unanswered. Again
Melancton Smith brought his stunned followers into line—
although there were witnesses who during the next two days
thought they detected in the Antifederalist leader's voice an
overtone of doubt. Nor did these same witnesses fail to notice that, during a subsequent afternoon, Governor Clinton
left the meeting room to spend an hour pacing the courthouse piazza, hands behind his back and on his rugged fea-
tures the expression of a man in the toils of inner struggle.

On July 4 the Federalists celebrated Independence Day in one of the town's taverns, the Antis in another, and Federalist John Jay canvassed the area, looking for a sorrel mare that some rascal, probably Antifederalist, had stolen from the stable he had rented for it.

During the week that followed Jay had little time for mourning his missing sorrel. On the eleventh he introduced a resolution calling on the convention to ratify the Constitution unconditionally. This action produced five days of noisy but fruitless debate. Then on July 15, Melancton Smith countered for the Antis by introducing a substitute resolution. Smith proposed that the convention ratify the Constitution conditionally by attaching to its endorsement a proviso permitting New York State to withdraw from the union unless within a reasonable time certain amendments were adopted.

Fearful that this was the best the Federalists could get from the convention, Hamilton sent a message by express rider to Madison, who had come up to New York City following the conclusion of the Virginia convention. Should he accept Smith's proposition, Hamilton asked, or should he fight on?

Madison's answer was on hand within the next twenty-four hours. He urged Hamilton to fight on. In Madison's opinion, Smith's proposition that New York reserve "a right to withdraw, if amendments be not decided on . . . within a certain time" would not make her "a member of the new Union . . . she could not be received on that plan." He added that the "Constitution requires an adoption *in toto* and *for ever*. It has been so adopted by the other states."

Hamilton fought on. In what one observer called "a most argumentative and impassioned address," he risked everything with a demand that the delegates either accept the Constitution or reject it. Let them, if they wished, accompany their acceptance with a list of the amendments they would like to see passed—but first of all let them accept it *"in toto* and *for ever."*

It was a phenomenal speech, probably the most effective one of Hamilton's life. Lawyer Kent, still breathlessly following every blow of the contest, did not regard Hamilton as a true orator. His voice was too light for those organ-like effects that passed for oratory in eighteenth-century America. Still there was a nervous intensity about him as a speaker, a sincerity, a relentless probing into the subject at hand that "proselytes the judgment." Another observer likened Hamilton on this occasion to a "political porcupine, armed at all points," his words combining "the poignancy of vinegar with the smoothness of oil." Still another found his "display of intellectual power" all "the more remarkable" because of "his total lack of faith in the plan," meaning in the Constitution he was defending. Federalist listeners took the recurrent murmurs of approval among the Antis as evidence that Hamilton's arguments were winning converts.

On Thursday, July 24, the break came. Rising from his place, speaking, as always, soberly and with deliberation, Melancton Smith switched sides.

On Friday, word of the Antifederalist leader's recantation reached New York City, and the people there poured into the streets for a giant patriotic rally. Feature of their long and gaudy parade was a mammoth float labeled "The Good Ship Alexander Hamilton."

On Saturday, the eleventh state, New York, ratified the Constitution. And not quite a year later, on April 30, 1789, Hamilton, from the window of his New York house at Broad and Wall streets, witnessed with pride the unprecedented occurrence taking place on the balcony of Federal Hall across the street—the inauguration of George Washington as first President of the United States.

7

Supernatural Thunders

Having acted as a midwife at the birth of the Federal government, Hamilton had no intention of entrusting its up-
bringing exclusively to others. When in the summer of
1789, the first Federal Congress, meeting in New York,
began setting up the executive departments of the new government, he let it be known that he was ready and willing to
oversee the development of American fiscal policy. Influential friends, Robert Morris among them, assured Washington that Hamilton was also able, and in the fall he became a
member of the President's five-man Cabinet, with the title
Secretary of the Treasury.

Probably few other men in the country could have coped
with the young Republic's tangled finances. Hamilton not
only swiftly unraveled them but did so with the ease and

style that makes the difficult look simple and that characterize the true professional. Within a few months, many men
who had questioned his qualifications in the beginning were
heeding his official statements "with as much confidence," to
quote one of them, "as if they had been delivered from
Mount Sinai, in the midst of supernatural thunders."

During the Revolution the Continental Congress had
borrowed huge sums from foreign nations, chiefly France
and Holland. It had also borrowed heavily from its own citizens, giving them in return I.O.U.'s commonly spoken of as
paper claims or certificates. Including overdue interest, the
national government's war debt came to about sixty-six million dollars. This was a staggering sum for an infant nation
with less than half a dozen banks, a scattering of small and
struggling industries, and not quite four million inhabitants, of whom ninety per cent were farmers and six per cent
slaves.

In the House of Representatives, where under the Constitution all money bills must originate, there were no disputes
as to what should be done about this obligation. The Republic could not hope to win a place of respect in the world
community unless it made good on its promises. The debt
must be paid. The question was how, and ten days after
Hamilton assumed his Cabinet post, the members of the
House called on him for an answer.

Their action came on the heels of a brief argument, one
that is of interest as foreshadowing the more tempestuous arguments to come. Should the Secretary give them the benefit
of his advice orally and in person, or should he draw up a
paper and send it to them by messenger? Fresh in the minds
of the members was the irresistible argumentation whereby
Hamilton, during his major speech at Poughkeepsie, had

cozened New York's overwhelmingly Antifederalist convention into ratifying the Constitution. The consensus of the
House was that the national lawmakers should not put
themselves in the humiliating position of being influenced
by the new Secretary's persuasive ways. Their formal resolution ordered him, whenever his answer was ready, to submit
it in writing.

He submitted it five months later, and the explosion that
followed could scarcely have been louder had the persuasive
Secretary himself been there to present it. It could be said
that on the day that Hamilton's famous "Report on the Public Credit" reached the floor of the House of Representatives
—January 14, 1790—America's two-party system was born.

The report drove a wedge through the House and, by ex-
tension, through the entire country. To one side stood the
pro-administration forces, the Federalists. To the other
stood the anti-administration forces, soon to be known as the
Republicans or the Democrats. Generally speaking, the Federalists found nothing particularly alarming in the report.
On the other hand, the Republicans* found little in it that
wasn't alarming. Within a fortnight two aspects of it had
become centers of a controversy in and out of Congress.

One aspect was the treasury head's proposal that in funding the domestic debt, the Federal government purchase the
claims against it—the outstanding certificates—from their
present holders, even if those holders were not the original
owners. What worried the Republicans about this arrange-

---

* A little reminder: Use of the word "Democrats," to designate the
members of the political party founded by Thomas Jefferson, did not
become common until after Hamilton's death. In other words, the
people referred to in this book as "Republicans" were actually Democrats and should not be confused with today's Republicans, whose
party dates from 1856.

ment was their belief that it would work a hardship on many one-time original holders who had disposed of their certificates. It would be especially unfair, the Republicans said, to veterans of the Revolutionary War who years before had received government certificates in lieu of the military pay due them and had subsequently sold their claims at a fraction of their face value.

A simple hypothetical case can be cited to crystallize the Republican argument. Suppose that on leaving the army in 1781, Soldier A accepted an interest-bearing certificate worth a hundred dollars in place of the wages due him. Suppose that in 1785, being pressed for money, he sold his certificate for sixty dollars to Wealthy Citizen B. Having no immediate need for cash, Citizen B had held the certificate ever since. If now Hamilton's suggested funding plan became law, Wealthy Citizen B would receive from the government one hundred dollars for a certificate that had cost him only sixty dollars.

How did the Republicans suggest getting around this "inequity," as they called it? They wanted the government to discriminate between original holders and so-called transferees or present holders. This would mean getting the name of every original holder and paying him the face value of the certificate less whatever he had sold it for. As for the transferee, he would receive the difference—the amount he had paid for the certificate. Interest due would be similarly apportioned, and if several transferees were involved only the last of them, the present holder of the certificate, would get a share.

With his usual thoroughness, Hamilton had anticipated the Republican objections to his domestic funding scheme and had answered them in his report. Discriminating between original holders and transferees, he pointed out, would be a phenomenally complex undertaking. In the case of veterans, the names of the original holders could be traced through military records. Where thousands of non-veterans were concerned, however, identifying the first holders would be time consuming, expensive, and frequently futile. His major point was that failure to pay the present certificate-holders in full would be a violation of contract. Those original owners who had sold their certificates had done so with the understanding that they were giving up all rights to them in return for the agreed-upon price. Those who had bought them had done so in good faith. Moreover, they had taken a risk, since at the time of the transfer they had no idea when, if ever, the government would redeem these claims. Behind Hamilton's every move as a public official was his vision of the America to come—a united and dynamic community rich with the fruits of an ever expanding commerce and an increasingly more productive industry. This dream, he proclaimed, could be realized only under a government that upheld the sanctity of contracts.

The other unsettling aspect of his "Report on the Public Credit" was his proposal that the Federal government do more than pay its own debts. He suggested that it also assume and fund the war debts still owed by the individual states.

This procedure would lift the Federal government's total payments to slightly more than eighty million dollars. The high sum the scheme called for did not trouble the Republican leaders; but its political implications did. Some of them had been delegates to the Federal convention in Philadelphia. They remembered how on that hot afternoon in 1787

Alexander Hamilton had expressed the hope that under the forthcoming Constitution the states would be stripped of their sovereignty. Later Hamilton had shifted ground, saying that he wished the states to retain the bulk of their powers. To his Republican foes, however, his original statement would always carry more conviction than his subsequent denials of it.

States' rights were as sacred to them as contracts were to him. They interpreted his assumption proposal as an attempt to diminish the importance of the states by forcing their citizen-creditors to turn for payment, not to them, but to the Federal government. Hamilton's answer to this charge was to admit and defend it. The Federal government, he argued, was young and struggling; it needed friends; the more creditors it satisfied, the more friends it would have.

In the House of Representatives, formal debate on the Secretary's report began on February 8 and continued during the rest of the winter, all spring, and well into the warm months. Gradually two bills emerged—the Funding Bill, dealing with the Federal debt; and the Assumption Bill, dealing with the debts of the states.

A favorite Republican contention was that, unless the Funding Bill discriminated between original certificate-holders and transferees, it would benefit the rich at the expense of the poor. Events during the spring and summer lent color to this argument. Speculators in New York and other financial centers, most of them certain that the bill would eventually pass, sent agents into the backwoods sections of the country with instructions to buy as many certificates as they could for as little money as sellers could be talked into accepting.

Naturally the Republicans blamed Hamilton for this de-

velopment. Their condemnation of the "storm of speculation" released by "the wicked friend of the New York money
kings" had a fine and righteous but, under the circumstances, rather hollow ring. Hamilton did not encourage the
speculators in any way. When a wealthy friend wrote, asking
him for information on progress of the debate over the
Funding Bill, the Secretary replied that he never discussed
the subject outside of official circles. "Like Caesar's wife," he
added, a public servant "must be above suspicion."

Inadvertently, on the other hand, his Republican adversaries were of considerable assistance to the "money kings."
Travel was snail-like in the eighteenth century. It took
weeks, even months, for the speculators' buying agents to
reach those remote areas of the country where news of the
Funding Bill had not yet penetrated. Hamilton, on submit-
ting his report, had hoped that Congress would act on it
quickly. Had Congress done so, the speculators could not
have created much havoc. The Republican leaders gave
them the time they needed by protracting the debate for almost eight months. Much of the summer had gone by before
the Funding Bill, written in accordance with Hamilton's report, became law on July 29, 1790.

At this point, its companion measure, the bill calling for
Federal assumption of state debts, was still in trouble. Early
in June the House had voted it down by a small margin.
Stunned by this defeat, Hamilton might have given up this
phase of his program had it not been for a debate over another issue then going forward.

The last Confederation Congress had chosen New York
City as the meeting place for the first Federal Congress.

Choice of a permanent capital, however, rested with the new Congress; and for months the question of where this should be located had provoked almost as much oratory as Hamilton's "Report on the Public Credit."

Congressmen from the predominantly Federalist northern and middle states wanted the capital in their area, Philadelphia being the city most frequently named. Those from the primarily Republican South had their hearts set on a site more convenient to their homes. To this end they had introduced a measure known as the Residence Bill calling for the national capital to stand on the Potomac River near the little Maryland city of Georgetown.

What intrigued Hamilton about this dispute was that the status of the Residence Bill was almost identical with that of the Assumption Bill. The fate of both proposals depended on what happened in the House of Representatives. There, in early June, the Southerners needed only a few Federalist votes to put the national capital where they wanted it. Similarly, Hamilton's followers needed only a few Republican votes to bring up the Assumption Bill for a second time and pass it.

It is not clear just when Hamilton began thinking seriously of a swap, a compromise. Neither is it clear whether he broached the subject by plan or on the spur of the moment when, in front of the President's house one morning, he chanced to meet the Secretary of State, Thomas Jefferson, whose close ties with the Republicans in Congress put him in position to persuade some of them to change their votes on assumption from nay to aye.

When President Washington expressed a desire to have Jefferson in his cabinet, the Virginian was still in France, where for five years he had attended to his country's dealings

with that nation. On his return to the United States in November of 1789, he was at first hesitant about accepting
Washington's invitation. He would have preferred returning to France or, better yet, simply remaining at Monticello,
the lovely hilltop home in Virginia that he himself had designed.

Unlike Hamilton, Jefferson never regarded public service
as the Alpha and Omega of life. The Virginian's interests
and talents spanned an incredible gamut—from agriculture
to architecture, from town planning to the etymology of the
languages of the American Indian. When in due time he
and Hamilton clashed in bitter political feud, the New
Yorker was fond of dismissing the Virginian's avowed aver-
sion to public office as "hypocrisy," a case of Jefferson slyly
sliding the velvet glove over the iron fist of power. Some of
Jefferson's appraisals of Hamilton's motives were equally bizarre—and unfounded. When early in 1790 Jefferson agreed
to serve as his country's first Secretary of State, his reluctance
about assuming his duties was genuine.

Although the quarrel between him and Hamilton was
destined to shake Washington's administration from top to
bottom, it did not emerge immediately. As fellow Cabinet
members they were thrown together almost daily, but for
some months their relationship was polite and congenial.
Never, however, was it genuinely friendly. More than political principle divided them. Physically, temperamentally—in
every way they were unlike.

Hamilton was a small compact man with auburn hair, fair
skin, and a face that was strikingly contradictory, with its
cold blue eyes and tender, mobile mouth. Only five-feet-
seven, he carried himself with a military erectness that made
him look far taller. Jefferson, a redhead, bony-faced and

sandy-complexioned, was a tall man who habitually slouched as though embarrassed by his height and at pains to minimize it. Hamilton was a fashion plate. Jefferson's clothes always looked too small for him. Even good friends complained that he carried too far the sartorial negligence considered forgivable in a philosopher.

Add to these external differences an even sharper internal difference. Jefferson, the "father of democracy," was shy and reserved in the presence of most people, a highly self-protective man with a genius for detachment. "The art of life," he wrote a close friend in Europe, "is the art of avoiding pain. . . . The most effectual means of being secure against pain, is to retire within ourselves. . . . Hence the inestimable value of intellectual pleasures [which permit us to leave] . . . the bustle and tumult of society to those who have no talents to occupy themselves without them." Hamilton, contrariwise, could no more remove himself from "the bustle and tumult of society" then he could sprout wings and fly. Notwithstanding his yearning for aristocracy and his hatred of democracy, he was warm in his relations with those around him and vulnerable to their opinions of him, with a tendency to become emotionally involved in their personal problems.

At the root of the political battle between these two remarkable men lay their sharply varying opinions of human nature. Both accepted the religious teaching that man has a dual nature, meaning that he is capable of both good and evil. Hamilton's conservatism was a natural outgrowth of his fear that, given freedom, men would do more evil than good. From this conviction flowed his desire for a strong national government run by "the rich, the educated and the good." It is vital to add that he wanted this government by the few to be conducted in the interests of the many. He believed in a paternalistic government, a managed national economy. Potentially his political ideas were close to the collectivist and welfare-state theories of the twentieth century.

Jefferson's liberalism drew sustenance from his belief that when men are given freedom along with education and economic opportunity, their better natures prevail and they govern themselves peacefully and well. Consistent with this view was his affection for states' rights, for spreading out the country's political powers so as to bring them closer to the people. His political philosophy was replete with the personal and economic individualism—the laissez-faire theories, that is—of the eighteenth and nineteenth centuries.

Of the many contributions that the two great rivals made to their country, probably none was as important as their quarrel itself. Compromise may be necessary to the progress of a free society, but differences cannot be fruitfully reconciled until someone comes along with enough forthrightness and wit to tell society what the differences are. Because Hamilton and Jefferson did this so well, each articulating his side of the argument with force and clarity, posterity has paid them its greatest tribute. Both are as alive to us today as when they walked the earth.

So much for some of the qualities and attitudes of the two men who, in New York City that June day in 1790, embarked on their first—and last—cooperative venture. According to Jefferson, Hamilton was not at his best that morning. Worry over the plight of the Assumption Bill had left its marks. The treasury secretary's "look was sombre, haggard and dejected . . . even his dress uncouth & neglected." Plainly his wits were not correspondingly awry, for he shrewdly refrained from suggesting a give-and-take arrangement that would hand the Southern Republicans what they wanted—a national capital on the Potomac—and the Federalists what they were looking for—Federal assumption of the states' debts. The whole of his conversation was a plea that Jefferson use his influence to rescue the Assumption Bill from defeat. Taking the Virginian by the arm, he walked him "backwards and forwards before the President's door for half an hour." He argued that only through assumption could the Republic save its credit abroad. He voiced the fear that if the project failed, some states would secede from the union.

The Virginian's response to these statements was to suggest that they discuss the matter further at a second meeting. This meeting took place the next day in the dining room of Jefferson's rented house on Maiden Lane. Three other men were present—Madison and two other members of the House of Representatives from Virginia. It was on this occasion that Jefferson, not Hamilton, proposed a compromise. He and Madison would undertake to get enough Southern votes to insure passage of the Assumption Bill. In return Hamilton was to solicit enough Federalist votes to pass the Residence Bill that the Southerners wanted.

All parties made good on their pledges. By the end of the first week of August both bills had become laws. The Residence Bill provided that for ten years, beginning in December of 1790, the seat of government would be Philadelphia. After that it would be a newly created Federal district on the Potomac, to be known as Washington, D.C.

In later years Jefferson regretted his part in the compromise of 1790. As with the passage of time he became his country's foremost states'-rightist, it embarrassed him to remember the pains he had taken to help Alexander Hamilton put over a bill designed to magnify the majesty of the Federal government and reduce that of the states. In an account of the incident written twenty years later, Jefferson accused Hamilton of taking advantage of the Virginian's long absence from the country and his consequent ignorance of its fiscal problems to mislead him concerning the nature of the Assumption Bill. But as a matter of fact, in 1790 Jefferson was no babe in the woods where his country's monetary affairs were concerned. Before leaving Europe he had helped persuade the Dutch bankers to lend money to the American states by assuring them that in time the Federal government would assume responsibility for their payment.

☆   ☆   ☆

Hamilton's "Report on the Public Credit" was only the first of several closely reasoned papers in which he called on Congress for the laws he considered essential to his grand scheme for placing the new Republic on a sound financial basis. The second of these now famous papers, his "Report on the National Bank," reached the floor of the House in September of 1790; the third, "Report on Establishment of a Mint," in January of 1791; the fourth, "Report on Manufactures," in December of that year; and the final paper, entitled "Second Report on the Public Credit" and written after its author had retired from the treasury, in January of 1795.

The reaction of the legislators to the "Report on the National Bank" was swift. In January of 1791, Congress passed and sent to the President a bill authorizing the government to charter a private institution that would be known later as the First Bank of the United States. At the executive mansion in Philadelphia, whence Congress had moved only a few weeks before, the bill encountered a delay while Washington pondered the contention of its Republican critics that Congress did not have the power to create such an institution.

As always, when faced with a ticklish problem, Washington asked his Cabinet members to submit their opinions in writing. Taking the Republican position, Jefferson wrote that nowhere in the Constitution was there so much as a phrase permitting Congress to establish a bank. He thus set forth his and his followers' belief in strict construction of the basic law of the land: unless that document gave Congress the power to do something in so many words, Congress could not do it.

Hamilton, rushing to the defense of a measure vital to his grand scheme, resorted to the doctrine of implied powers. The Constitution, he argued, empowered Congress to further the "general welfare of the nation." It followed that Congress could do whatever was necessary to achieve that goal.

Sixty-two years later, the treasury secretary's widow, Betsey Schuyler Hamilton, would offer a delightful version of how this argument, America's first constitutional crisis, was resolved. "Jefferson thought we ought not to have a bank," she would recall, "and President Washington thought so. But my husband said, We must have a Bank. I sat up all night, copied out his writing, and the next morning he carried it to President Washington and we had a Bank." We "had" it on January 25, 1791, when Washington signed the controversial bill into law.

Generally speaking, Congress responded favorably to all of Hamilton's major propositions. With the opening of the United States mint in Philadelphia in 1792, his grand financial scheme stood practically complete.

Large numbers of Americans liked it and for good reason

since it provided the Republic with badly needed economic strength. The Republicans, however, remained unreconciled. To them the creation of a national bank outside of the government established a reservoir of power that only the affluent could tap. They said that the bank and other elements of the program encouraged the "evil of speculation." Southern Republicans, making this charge, were careful to define as "evil" only speculation in governmental securities or other forms of financial paper. Presumably, the kind of speculation then rampant below the Potomac, speculation in land, existed on another and more virtuous level.

To such Republican philosophers as Jefferson and his friend Madison, the grand scheme channeled too much power into the Federal government, and especially into the executive branch. As for the man responsible for it, he was the "colossus of monocrats," in Jefferson's phrase. Hamilton might not be trying to impose a king on the American people, but he was certainly pushing the Federal establishment as close to a monarchy as a kingless government could get.

To many Republicans the grand scheme was not as reprehensible as the high-handed manner in which its architect achieved it. Jefferson was stating simple fact when he complained that Hamilton did not think of himself as merely one of Washington's confidential advisers. He thought of himself as "prime minister," the man in charge of everything, subject only to the will of his presidential chief. To be sure, he sent to Congress only such recommendations as that body requested. Having proposed a course of action, however, he proceeded to oversee its progress through the torturous legislative mill, from inception to passage. He obtained the appointment of committees sympathetic to his financial plans, and when the time came to vote, he counted heads and marshaled his forces as if he himself were sitting in Congress as an elected member. Republican critics jibed, mournfully, that the government could have saved itself considerable money by simply dismissing Congress and letting Alexander Hamilton handle that aspect of things along with his treasury duties.

Even within the President's cabinet, Hamilton refused to confine himself to his own bailiwick. Repeatedly, secretly— and at points dishonorably—he invaded Jefferson's department in an effort to manipulate American foreign policy.

The infant Republic's relations with the Old World were precarious. The French Revolution, the emergence of the first French republic, the revival of old disputes among the European nations and the eruption of new ones—these events presented Washington and Jefferson with hard problems. As leaders of a new and militarily unprepared country, it behooved them to move warily. This they did, struggling determinedly to maintain an attitude of neutrality toward the quarreling powers across the sea.

It was this sensible policy that Hamilton, operating behind the scenes, tried for a period to overturn. A frequent visitor to the national capital was George Beckwith, a seasoned confidential agent of the British government. Beckwith's mission was to sound out American sentiment, to determine how much of it was favorable to his country. He found Hamilton sympathetic and conversed with him often in the privacy of the Secretary's office. In reporting a portion of these conversations to the President, Hamilton withheld some facts and falsified others in an attempt to woo Washington from his neutral position to one more friendly to Great Britain. Neither the President nor Jefferson suspected what the treasury head was doing. Fortunately for the country, neither of them was influenced by his misleading reports.

By no means all of Hamilton's attempts to shape his country's foreign policy were conducted in this cloak-and-dagger fashion. Most of his exertions in this field were legitimate, and some were beneficial. Washington often asked his advice on dealing with other nations. This was particularly true after December of 1793, when Jefferson retired from the Cabinet and the competent but less creative Edmund Randolph of Virginia succeeded him as Secretary of State.

In 1794 the new Republic at last succeeded in obtaining a badly needed treaty of commerce with Great Britain. The agreement required that England surrender the outposts that her soldiers had been occupying in the American Northwest. Some of its other terms were advantageous to the United States, but many were not. On the contrary, they made such drastic concessions to Great Britain that even after all but one article had been ratified by the Senate, the document continued for years to be a source of controversy. So pervasive was Hamilton's role, first in negotiating this agreement and then in defending it, that in the opinion of many of his contemporaries, Jay's Treaty, as the agreement was known, should have been called Hamilton's Treaty.

☆   ☆   ☆

Since in the eighteenth century travel was slow and dangerous, politicians made little effort to disseminate their respective gospels by going on speaking tours as they would later. Instead they warred on one another in the press. In bringing his fiscal program to fruition, Hamilton found an invaluable ally in John Fenno, publisher-editor of the *Gazette of the United States,* largest of Philadelphia's twelve newspapers and the only American newspaper to come close to having a national circulation.

A militant Federalist, Fenno used every trick of his trade to persuade his readers that as both a man and a public official, Alexander Hamilton was only a trifle short of divine. On the other hand, his castigation of the treasury secretary's foes and especially of Thomas Jefferson was pursued with a virulence that sometimes put a strain even on John Fenno's munificent vocabulary of epithet.

Unlike his touchy rival, Jefferson was inclined to be philosophic about such attacks. Even so, he soon realized that unless he and his adherents found a liberal organ as effective as Fenno's conservative *Gazette of the United States,* their struggle for a more democratic America would be lost by default. In the fall of 1791, Jefferson persuaded Philip Freneau of New York, the "Poet of the Revolution" and a confirmed anti-Hamiltonian, to move to Philadelphia and found a Republican newspaper called the *National Gazette.*

A master of the scurrilous phrase, Freneau proved the perfect foil to Fenno. In the columns of the poet's *National Gazette,* Hamilton became the "arch-enemy of Republicanism," a "criminal" bent on entrapping the nation in "a web of speculative and monarchial influence." The pen that oozed vitriol also had honey in it. To the editor of the *National Gazette,* Jefferson was always "the Colossus of Liberty . . . that illustrious Patriot, Statesman and Philosopher."

Stung by Freneau's attacks and even more annoyed by his deification of Jefferson, Hamilton did some detective work and came up with a plum. Freneau, he discovered, had been reluctant about moving to Philadelphia. To lure him there Jefferson had given him a job as a translating clerk in the Department of State. In a brace of newspaper articles, Hamilton first hinted and then charged that Jefferson was using taxpayer's money to persecute him—Hamilton—"for the unpardonable sin of having been the steady, invariable and decided friend of broad national principles of government."

Freneau, counterattacking quickly, took the line that, in making this charge, the treasury head was throwing stones from a glass house. Was it not "common knowledge" that since the removal of the government to Philadelphia, Hamilton had channeled all of his department's printing to Federalist Fenno's shop? Was it not also evident that articles appearing in Fenno's paper over such sobriquets as "Catullus" and "Scourge" were actually the product of the treasury secretary himself?

So it went, the Republican hammer clanging and the Federalist tong replying. The outbreak of the French Revolution introduced a new and more strident note into the quarrel. Indeed this event did as much as Hamilton's financial program to divide the country into factions. Taking their cue from Jefferson, the Republicans saw in the French upheaval, with all its excesses, a great leap forward in mankind's struggle for freedom. Like all Federalists, Hamilton had eyes only for the excesses. The execution of the French king and queen, the Reign of Terror, and later the emergence of the dictator Napoleon—to Hamilton these abrasive developments were living examples of the evils awaiting the nation that puts its faith in democracy.

When editor Freneau ran out of other belittling expressions, he could always delight his Republican readers by picturing Hamilton as suffering from "Anglomany," the dread disease of those bent on recreating the Federal government in the image and likeness of the British parliamentary system that Hamilton so admired. Editor Fenno could always freeze the blood of his Federalist readers by describing Jefferson as "that Frenchified philosopher" who, according to Hamilton, loved revolution for its own sake and was "prone to projects incompatible with the principles of stable and systematic government."

So long as the Republicans confined their criticisms to Hamilton's political views—his approval of the British form of government and his distaste for democracy—they were on sound ground. When, however, they accused him of using his high office for personal gain, they displayed a woeful ignorance of the character of their archenemy. They also treated their countrymen to an array of undignified extravaganzas.

8

Fox Hunt

☆   ☆   ☆

In both his private and public life Alexander Hamilton was a paragon of financial rectitude. It is still another commentary on his contradictory nature that this man who did so much to make other Americans wealthy never showed any interest in becoming wealthy himself. The father of the profit motive was not interested in profits. Fame, glory, and, above all, the satisfaction of having done something constructive for his country—these, not money, were the spurs that drove Alexander Hamilton.

His acceptance of the treasury post was a serious sacrifice. As one of the country's best lawyers, he could count on a yearly income of ten thousand dollars, a large sum in his day. His three-thousand-dollar-a-year salary as a Cabinet member barely met the needs of a family that by 1792 included five children ranging in age from nine years to a few weeks.

At one point the man responsible for collecting his country's taxes and managing its eighty-million-dollar debt had to borrow twenty dollars from a friend to take care of current personal expenses. The lender was truly a friend in need; he sent the impoverished Secretary a check for fifty dollars. In 1794 a French visitor to Hamilton's office in Philadelphia could hardly believe his eyes. He estimated the furnishings of the little room to be worth at most only ten dollars. The Secretary's filing cabinets consisted of planks laid on trestles. His desk was a common pine table covered with a green cloth.

Neither the simplicity of Hamilton's office nor the leanness of his own purse made any impression on his political enemies. For those who feel they have no part in it nothing annoys like success. As one by one Congress converted the elements of Hamilton's grand financial scheme into law, it became an article of faith among his critics that he was enriching himself by sharing his special knowledge of the country's fiscal plans with the greedy "money-kings" of New York and Philadelphia. By 1791 their search for evidence of "vile corruption" in the treasury department had taken on the trappings of a fox hunt with the Republican hounds in full cry.

Late that year some Indians took to the warpath in the Northwest Territory, and Henry Knox, as Secretary of War, ordered Major General Arthur St. Clair to put down the disturbance. Hamilton's suggestion that St. Clair use soldiers belonging to the regular army drew a howl from Republican leaders in Congress. They were sick and tired, they said, of the treasury secretary's unflagging efforts to see to it that the Federal government got all the glory. They insisted that St.

Clair's fighting force consist entirely of militia drawn from the states. Knox bowed to their wishes; and St. Clair and his militia hastened west, met the Indians on the shores of the Wabash, and were ignominiously defeated.

Undaunted, the Republicans made a strenuous effort to put the blame for this fiasco on Hamilton. They pointed out that some of the supplies intended for St. Clair had failed to reach him and that the treasury secretary had prepared the requisite contracts. Putting these facts together, they concluded that Hamilton had handled the contract negotiations dishonestly, and demanded an investigation.

They got it—and regretted it. Examination of the records showed that whatever had gone wrong was the fault not of Hamilton but of the Secretary of War. The findings further indicated that the expedition might have succeeded had St. Clair used regular soldiers as the treasury secretary had suggested.

The Republican hunting hounds were discouraged—but not for long. In the autumn of 1792 their fox stumbled. Two years before, Congress had authorized President Washington to borrow fourteen million dollars from Europe. The lawmakers recommended that this money be used for certain specific purposes, but Hamilton had applied some of it to other legal but quite different purposes. Then in November of 1792 he suggested that the lawmakers empower him to pay in full one of the country's larger domestic debts, using money drawn from the funds he had borrowed abroad. This revelation by Hamilton himself that he was not using the borrowed funds precisely as Congress wished put the Republican hunting hounds into full cry again. They instructed the treasury secretary to give Congress a statement describing exactly what he had done with the funds. When the statement arrived, they pronounced it "inaccurate, defective and imperfect" and accused Hamilton of deliberately keeping Congress in the dark about what was going on in his department.

This charge was not without basis. The law making it mandatory for the treasury secretary to send annual reports to Congress had not yet been passed. All the Constitution required was that "from time to time" he publish an "account of the receipts and expenditures of . . . public money." With characteristic high-handedness, Hamilton interpreted "from time to time" to mean whenever he felt like it, which was seldom. When he did give the lawmakers a report, he couched it in general terms on the condescending but not necessarily inaccurate assumption that most of them wouldn't understand the details anyhow.

The Republicans understood one thing clearly: something was rotten in the treasury department and the time had come to root it out. Having learned that Hamilton was a hard fox to snare, they proceeded cautiously. Their first step was to prevail upon Congress to name a committee to examine the affairs of the treasury department. The members of the committee questioned officials of the department, scrutinized its transactions with the country's private financial institutions, and even inspected Hamilton's personal bank accounts. What they were looking for was evidence that he had used public money for his own speculations or for the purchase of votes in Congress, or both.

What they dug up was nothing. Finding Hamilton innocent of dishonesty, they fell back on the only charge still available to them—that in disbursing the money borrowed abroad he had not always followed the recommendations of Congress. The task of converting this trifling charge into a set of resolutions and of getting the House of Representatives to pass them fell to young William B. Giles.

Of average height, with a full squat figure and a big round colorless face, this virile planter-politican from Virginia was famous for his accomplishments as a debater, his admiration for "canvas-back ducks, ham and chickens, old Madeira," and all the other "glories of the Ancient Dominion," his consumption of wine and cherry bounce, and his abiding certainty that Alexander Hamilton and the Devil were one and the same. In short, he was the ideal man to prosecute the Republicans' case against the Secretary of the Treasury on the floor of the House.

He enjoyed the assistance of an even more capable man. Hamilton was correct in his often voiced suspicion that a good deal of the strategy behind the assault on his personal integrity came from Thomas Jefferson. As a political leader, the Secretary of State was much given to working behind the scenes, to drawing up plans and then letting other men carry them out on the firing line—a prudent procedure that Hamilton, with his passion for combat and danger, seldom followed.

In the quiet of his study Jefferson drew up a tentative list of resolutions. Cavalierly ignoring the failure of the Congressional investigators to turn up any evidence of dishonesty by Hamilton, he pointed to "unexplained shortages" in the treasury secretary's accounts, accused him of "maladministration," and urged Congress to declare him unfit for public office. Even to Giles, devoted as he was to the cause, these statements were a shade stiff. He softened them. In their final form, eight of Giles' resolutions merely rang changes on the Republican contention that Hamilton was running the treasury department his way instead of Congress' way. The ninth and final resolution proposed that Congress submit to the President a review of the Secretary's "crimes," an action equivalent to asking Washington to dismiss him.

Giles' resolutions were ready early in 1792, but the Republicans deliberately refrained from presenting them until the session of Congress, then underway, was almost over. They used the intervening weeks to drum up support for their position. They also persuaded Congress to ask for another report from Hamilton. This time the lawmakers did not limit their request to an account of the Secretary's employment of the funds borrowed abroad. They demanded detailed information concerning every operation undertaken by his department since its inception almost four years before.

From their standpoint this was a shrewd move. The labors they had imposed on the treasury head were Herculean. They were sure that he could not complete them during the current session of Congress. They were hopeful that even some of the Federalists would take his failure to do so as a sign of guilt.

Unhappily for the Republican cause, Hamilton was quite capable of sitting up most of the night for many nights. Presumably his devoted Betsey sat up with him and "copied out his writing." When on February 27, 1792, only three days before the end of the session, Giles presented his resolutions, Hamilton's gigantic résumé of his department had been in the hands of the members of the House for several days.

It would appear that even some of the Republicans read it. At any rate, a number of them joined with the Federalists to vote down the first three resolutions almost as fast as Giles could introduce them. At this point Giles offered to withdraw the rest. This the triumphant Federalists would not hear of, and in short order all nine resolutions went crashing to defeat.

End of the efforts by Hamilton's foes to destroy his financial program by proving its creator corrupt? Not quite. Before the year 1792 was over, one of the most influential Republican members of the House, Frederick A. Muhlenberg of Pennsylvania, was in possession of information that convinced him that at last he and his fellow hunters were about to bag their fox.

☆   ☆   ☆

Muhlenberg's information came to him from a small-time Philadelphia businessman and part-time crook named Jacob Clingman, who at one time had been in the employ of the Pennsylvania Congressman. Some months before, Federal authorities had discovered that Clingman and his business partner, James Reynolds, had cheated a number of Revolutionary War veterans out of money that the government owed them. Reynolds had been released from prison on bail, but Clingman was still confined when, in the late fall of 1792, he got word to Muhlenberg that he and Reynolds could provide proof that Alexander Hamilton was indeed the "great embezzler" his political foes considered him to be. Clingman sent Muhlenberg only enough of his alleged proof to whet the Congressman's appetite. He promised further and more damaging revelations if Muhlenberg would use his influence to free him from jail.

Muhlenberg showed Clingman's communication to two of his Republican brethren, Senator James Monroe of Virginia and Representative Abraham Venable, also of Virginia. Together the three statesmen visited the Philadelphia jail for a talk with Clingman. From there they went to the modest Market Street residence where James Reynolds lived with his attractive young wife, whose first name was Maria.

At the Reynolds' home they cast their eyes on documents calculated to stir their Republican blood. James Reynolds showed them personal checks made out to him and signed by the treasury head. Why had the Secretary given him these sums? Because, as his political opponents had long suspected, Hamilton was using government funds to enrich himself by buying and selling government securities. From time to time Reynolds had acted as his agent in these speculations. The checks he had received were his payment for withholding Hamilton's "guilty secret" from the world.

So impressive were Reynolds' documents and so convincing his explanation of them that the three Republicans' first impulse was to take their findings directly to President Washington. Second and soberer thoughts prevailed. They decided instead to go first to Hamilton himself.

Why this procedure? It may have occurred to them that Reynolds and Clingman, the sources of their evidence against the Secretary, had lied to people before. Perhaps, being gentlemen, they thought Hamilton should have an opportunity to present his side of the story. Perhaps, being politicians, they could not put off for another moment the exquisite pleasure of seeing the "great embezzler" squirming before them.

In any event, to Hamilton they went; to that small and crudely furnished office on Chestnut Street, Philadelphia.

Monroe and Venable said little during this dramatic encounter. Muhlenberg spoke for them. He showed Hamilton the checks that Reynolds had received from the treasury head and peremptorily accused him of malfeasance in office. Hamilton's immediate reaction was an outburst of indignation. Then his tone changed and his voice fell as it came to him that he must do more than merely deny the Republican trio's charges. Once and for all he must demolish their suspicions concerning his integrity as a public servant. Otherwise they would destroy not only him but his grand scheme, the elaborate financial program he had developed as Secretary of the Treasury. That, in his opinion, would be a national disaster.

Hamilton's appraisal of what he had done for his country was scarcely a modest one; neither, in the eyes of history, was it an incorrect one. Without his grand financial scheme, the infant Republic might never have survived its growing pains. Clamping a tight rein on his anger, he told the Republican trio that Reynolds had falsified the significance of the money he had received from Hamilton. If Muhlenberg, Monroe, and Venable would come to the Secretary's house that night, he would tell them the truth and support his statements with written evidence.

When the three Republicans arrived at Hamilton's Philadelphia home, they did not find the Secretary alone. With him was his chief assistant in the treasury office, Oliver Wolcott of Connecticut. Hamilton had taken Wolcott into his confidence, and the New England statesman was on hand as a Federalist witness to the confrontation that followed.

It was an embarrassing evening for all concerned. Hamilton's first step was to turn over to his political enemies a number of letters that James Reynolds' young wife had written to him. One look at these and his accusers realized that they had been right in assuming that the treasury secretary had a "guilty secret." It was not, however, the kind of secret they were hunting for. The documents Hamilton had handed them were love letters.

The letters in themselves told them everything. Hamilton need not have added a word of explanation; but he did. Determined to set the record straight, he gave them a complete account of what future Americans would call the Reynolds Affair.

One summer day in 1791, Hamilton revealed, Mrs. Reynolds had come to his Chestnut Street office. No description of Maria Reynolds has come down to us, but it is clear that Alexander Hamilton found her attractive. No doubt her pretty eyes were moist and her lips atremble as she poured out her sad story.

She pictured herself as a woman in grave distress and in desperate financial need. She said that her home was New York City. Recently, however, her husband had deserted her, fleeing to Philadelphia and leaving her responsible for his many debts. She had come to the Quaker City "in an endeavor to reclaim the prodigal" and make him "do right" by his creditors and his wife.

Hamilton did not have to tell his Republican interrogators that he was an easy mark for hard-luck stories, even for one as palpably trumped up as this one. His generosity was common knowledge. During his law-practice days, professional associates had chided him repeatedly for the frequency with which he took on clients unable to pay. It seemed to his friend Robert Troup that Hamilton exerted as much effort to keep poor as most men did to make themselves rich. Troup once voiced the prophetic fear that if Hamilton failed to mend his ways in this regard he would die a pauper and be buried at public expense.

Hamilton was touched by Maria Reynolds' tale. He was

also intrigued by her obvious willingness to be more than friendly to any benefactor. He told her that he did not have on hand the amount of money she needed. He would be glad to bring it to her, however, after working hours. She gave him her Market Street address, and that night Maria Reynolds became the Secretary's mistress.

The remainder of the Reynolds Affair was equally pathetic and shabby. In due time, James Reynolds came storming into the Secretary's office. He said his wife had confessed all. He described himself as surprised and mortified. He threatened to tell Mrs. Hamilton of her husband's unfaithfulness—unless, of course, the Secretary could see his way to "lending" him some money.

At this point Hamilton realized that he was the victim of an extortion scheme. Maria Reynolds had lied to him. She and her husband, working together, had put him in a position where he must either meet Reynolds' demands or run the risk of humiliating his family. His checks to James Reynolds had nothing to do with the treasury department. They were his payments to a blackmailer.

As Hamilton had anticipated, his Republican listeners accepted his story implicitly—all of them, that is, except Senator Monroe, that capable but strangely colorless Virginian who would one day be President of the United States. Monroe's reservations, however, were couched in the vague language of a man who having been convinced against his will was of the same opinion still; and he did not press them. Five years later Hamilton would have reason to recall the dour Virginian's doubts, but for the time being he was content. On the morning after the confrontation at his home, he drew up a memorandum, covering the highlights of the Reynolds Affair and incorporating the promise of the statesmen with whom he had shared his guilty secret to keep it to themselves. To this document all of those involved, including Monroe, put their signatures.

When slightly more than two years later, on January 31, 1795, Hamilton left his post to return to his law practice in New York City, he was under the comfortable illusion that his secret was buried forever. Perhaps it would have been had his retirement from the treasury been also a retirement from politics; but it wasn't. Out of office, he continued to be as politically active as ever, with many Americans regarding him as the real, as distinct from the merely titular, head of the Federalist party. As such he remained a target for attack, especially from men unscrupulous enough to capitalize on the human weaknesses of prominent public figures.

9

"Mine is an odd destiny"

☆　☆　☆

Back to New York went Hamilton in the winter of 1795, back to the city he called home to resume his law practice and to settle his family in a fine house on Broadway. His expressed reason for leaving the government was a need to replenish an empty purse. Only to his friend Robert Troup did he reveal the true state of his finances. Far from enriching himself during his treasuryship, as his critics charged, he had impoverished himself. His personal debts, at the time of his resignation, were close to thirty thousand dollars.

In New York his practice flourished. Once more he dealt largely in civil matters, taking on an occasional criminal action. He and Aaron Burr were associated in the defense of Levi Weeks, a carpenter accused of brutally slaying a young woman under circumstances that made the Levi Weeks case America's first full-fledged murder mystery.

Tradition credits Hamilton with getting the carpenter off by the dramatic manner in which he cross-examined the chief witness for the prosecution. As Hamilton put his questions, he held a lighted candle in his hand. In its flickering flame the expressions on the witness' face clearly belied what he was saying. This device so undermined his testimony that the jury could only declare the defendant innocent and stamp the case "unsolved." Some purveyors of this tale credited Burr with the candle trick, and that cagey gentleman was certainly capable of it. Both he and Hamilton, however, were daringly inventive in the courtroom. Perhaps they dreamed it up together.

Heavy as Hamilton's practice was, life was not all work for him. As a private citizen he could indulge in "felicities," as he called them, that his secretarial labors had left him no time to enjoy. He was an amateur artist. He did a good deal of painting himself. He wrote long letters to Martha Washington, guiding her in the selection of paintings for the President's house in Philadelphia and for Mount Vernon, the Washingtons' farm home in Virginia. To his own collection of rare prints he added "a set of Montegna's superb chiarooscuro of the 'Triumph of Caesar' and a particularly fine Durer." He had a rich singing voice. Sometimes in the evenings he would entertain family and guests with it while Angelica, the oldest of his daughters, accompanied him on the piano or harp.

Guests came and went. The rich and the famous of both the Old World and the New, when they visited New York, gravitated to the Hamilton home. A frequent and welcome visitor was Angelica Schuyler Church, one of Betsey's older sisters. As sophisticated and stylish as Betsey was simple and dowdy, Angelica in her youth had eloped from home to marry an adventurous Englishman whose real name was unknown even to her family at that time. Later her shocked parents had taken consolation from learning that Angelica's husband, John Barker Church, came of respectable stock and was a genius at making money.

The Churches lived intermittently in America and Europe, but to Angelica the only good place to live was wherever Alexander Hamilton happened to be. She called him "my amiable" and "mon petit fripon," my little rogue. Her letters to Betsey were either paeans of praise for his brilliant mind and engaging conversation or anxious questions about his never robust health and his plans. And the fashionable ladies of New York, especially those with time on their hands, could always pass a pleasurable hour gossiping about "the shameless way that Angelica Church throws herself at her sister's husband."

In after years, the third oldest of Hamilton's sons, James Alexander, would draw an enticing picture of the early morning routine in the big Hamilton home on Broadway. "I distinctly recollect the scene at breakfast in the front room . . . ," he would write, "mother . . . at the head of the table with a napkin in her lap, cutting slices of bread, while the younger boys, . . . standing at her side, read in turn a chapter in the Bible or a portion of Goldsmith's 'Rome.' When the lessons were finished . . . father and the elder children were called to breakfast, after which the boys were packed off to school."

Sunday morning found the family in their pew at Trinity Church at the head of Wall Street. For New Yorkers, as for all American city dwellers in Hamilton's day, Sunday afternoon was promenade time. Weather permitting, the Hamiltons—father, mother, and children—joined the sedately strolling crowds on Broadway. Northward they would move, with Hamilton's three-cornered hat more frequently off than on as he acknowledged the greetings of passing friends and acquaintances. Past the open-air market at Maiden Lane they would saunter; past such local landmarks as the Poorhouse, the Gaol, the Theatre, and the gallows; past The Fields under whose giant sycamore and walnut trees Hamilton years ago had delivered the speech that had launched his public career. On a winter day, having reached the upper limits of the city, they would climb a one-hundred-foot hill and stand awhile on its farther slope, looking down on the skaters flashing across the surface of Collect Pond, or Fresh Water Pond, that once stood in what is now a section of the city's Lower East Side.

To the Republicans, the retired finance minister was still "the great embezzler" and the "colossus of monocrats." Among the citizens of his home town, however, he was an admired figure. It was not alone the merchants and shippers and professional men who appreciated the fruits of his grand financial scheme. From a long postwar depression the country had climbed to its greatest prosperity to date. Jobs were plentiful, wages high; and the laborers and shopkeepers of New York were aware that it was Alexander Hamilton who had so plentifully buttered their bread.

When the local merchants sponsored a public dinner in his honor at the Tontine Coffee House, well-brushed homespun mingled with the newly bought silks and satin of the affluent. It was a lavish affair: three hundred guests and numerous speakers. Nothing better attests the hardiness of our ancestors than their ability to consume a twelve-course meal, participate in twenty toasts, listen to as many after-dinner speeches, and still have enough strength at the end of the festivities to greet the last toast of all—to "Alexander Hamilton, Benefactor of Mankind"—with "three prolonged cheers."

☆   ☆   ☆

The American people might have been less quick to endorse the Constitution of 1787 had it not been a foregone conclusion that George Washington would serve as first President. Elected unanimously to his first term, the great soldier-statesman soon discovered what all of his successors would rediscover—that the presidency, in the phrase of his Vice President, John Adams of Massachusetts, was "a splendid misery." It was with deep reluctance, in 1792, that he agreed to stand for reelection and serve again. Consequently, those in the know were not altogether surprised when in the summer of 1796, with the third national election coming up in the fall, he declared that he would not accept a third term.

Although Hamilton had been expecting it, this announcement filled him with foreboding. He and Washington had never been convivial friends. But they had been close and amazingly like-minded collaborators for almost two decades. Hamilton had come to regard the thoughtful and unselfish Virginian as one of America's two indispensable institutions—the other one of course being his own grand financial scheme.

Sadly he performed what was to be his last important service for his chief. He helped him organize and write his famous Farewell Address. Published in September, this noble document urged Americans to stand aloof from troubles abroad and to avoid divisiveness at home. For a century United States foreign policy would hew to the line of Washington's words, but his warning against divisiveness at home overlooked his countrymen's need for political organizations through which to express their varying views on how the Republic should be run.

Already the ferment of divisiveness, of "faction" as Washington called it, was at work. Even as Americans read his final message to them, the Republican and Federalist leaders were preparing for the first presidential election whose outcome could not be foreseen.

In 1796, as would be true for almost forty more years, the candidates for the nation's top offices were not chosen at big nominating conventions. The principal method used was the so-called caucus. Party leaders simply got together and selected a couple of candidates. Since prior to 1804 the Constitution neglected to authorize the Electoral College to vote separately for President and Vice President, the members of the caucus usually refrained from making this distinction. Among themselves, however, and among their more alert followers, there was always a clear understanding as to which of their two candidates they hoped the people, acting through the Electoral College, would elevate to the presidency.

In the summer of 1796 the Republicans, caucusing in Philadelphia, named Jefferson as their presidential candidate and Aaron Burr for the vice presidency. The Federalists, also meeting in the Quaker City, chose as their presidential and vice presidential nominees, John Adams of Massachusetts and Thomas Pinckney of South Carolina.

To Hamilton this action by his fellow Federalists was almost as dispiriting as Washington's decision to step down. John Adams for President indeed! As the retired Secretary saw him, the crusty and deeply learned New Englander, with his variegated crotchets and swollen ego, was almost as "Frenchified" and therefore unsound in his views as the "great demagogue," to use Hamilton's favorite epithet for Jefferson.

Adams had occupied the vice presidency throughout the

Washington administration. From this exalted post—"the most insignificant . . . that ever invention of man contrived," as he himself described it—he had from time to time dropped sharply disapproving comments on the treasury secretary's grand financial scheme.

More to the point, Adams was a man of singular independence of mind. There were those who said Hamilton's break with him in 1796 was an outgrowth of his disappointment at being passed over for the presidency himself. That Hamilton harbored presidential ambitions* can be assumed; that they were relatively mild ones can also be assumed. He was never strongly attracted by the trappings of power. What he liked was power itself, and that, he had learned during Washington's administration, can be wielded from behind the presidential chair, so to speak. He knew John Adams well. He realized that if the rotund Massachusetts patriot ever caught anyone behind *his* chair, he would remove him forthwith!

On the other hand, Thomas Pinckney, the South Carolinian whom the Federalist chieftains had picked as their vice presidential nominee, was a man of another stripe: not so distinguished as Adams, to be sure; but genial, flexible, and unquestioningly Hamiltonian; in short, an ideal President in the eyes of a New York attorney determined in the future as the past to exert a substantial influence on the policies of his country. Making ample use of the United States mails, Hamilton proceeded to urge Federalist leaders in key states to manipulate the voting in the Electoral College so as to leave Adams where he was, in the vice presidency, and put Pinckney in the retiring President's place.

---

* Although born in the West Indies, he could have run. "No Person," the Constitution reads, "except a natural born citizen, *or a citizen of the United States, at the time of the adoption of this constitution,* shall be eligible to the Office of President . . ." Emphasis supplied.

Hamilton had made political mistakes before. He would make others in the future. Few of them, however, were as disastrous as this attempt to thwart the will of the other leaders of his party. When Adams caught wind of it, his anger initiated a division in the party ranks, a schism that a few years later would be heavily instrumental in bringing about first the decline and then the extinction of the Federalists as a political entity.

Even the short-range effects of Hamilton's maneuver were hardly what he had hoped for. In spite of his exertions to the contrary, Adams was elected to the presidency. In addition, such manipulation of the Electoral College as Hamilton succeeded in achieving had the stunning effect of eliminating Thomas Pinckney altogether and of catapulting the "great demagogue from Virginia" into the vice presidency. Indeed, according to John Quincy Adams, the new President's son, Jefferson would have won the presidency in 1796 had not the French minister to the United States campaigned for him in an open way—an attempt by the agent of a foreign country to interfere in an American election that did not set well with the American voters.

All in all, 1796 was a bad year for Hamilton. Even worse was the one that followed, for it was in the early months of 1797 that he discovered, with a sickening jolt, that his guilty secret, the Reynolds Affair, far from being dead and buried, was still embarrassingly alive.

☆   ☆   ☆

It will be recalled that, following Hamilton's revelation of his secret to three of his political opponents in 1792, all of them—Muhlenberg, Venable, and Monroe—solemnly agreed to keep it to themselves. Muhlenberg and Venable were as good as their word. Monroe was not. He told Jefferson about the Reynolds Affair almost immediately. He also made a transcription of Hamilton's confession. This record, along with other documents pertinent to the Reynolds Affair, he turned over—for safekeeping, he said—to another friend, named John James Beckley. Monroe was correct in assuming that Jefferson would not betray Alexander Hamilton's secret. It is hard to believe, however, that he was unaware that he was placing that secret in highly untrustworthy hands when he passed it on to John Beckley.

An ardent Republican and an equally ardent anti-Hamiltonian, Beckley was a minor political figure whose colorful career was to earn him the distinction of being the most effective "undercover political strategist of his day." Born in Virginia, he received his education at Eton in England and at the College of William and Mary in Williamsburg, Virginia, where he was a member of the original Phi Beta Kappa Society, founded there in 1776. Other small but gratifying distinctions were to befall him. Late in life he became the first librarian of what is now the Library of Congress, and today a small city in West Virginia bears his name.

In April of 1789 Beckley became the first clerk of the United States House of Representatives. This was a valuable position for a man whose fondness for intrigue brought him into close association with such unsavory characters as James Reynolds, his partner Clingman, and James T. Callender, a Scottish-born practitioner of what used to be called yellow journalism. When the Federalists contrived to have Beckley dismissed from his clerkship, he decided to strike back at them through their leader.

This objective he accomplished by simply turning over to journalist Callender the documents on the Reynolds Affair that James Monroe had confided to his care. Placing these damaging records in Callender's hands, he told the newspaperman to use them as he saw fit.

Callender knew exactly how to use them. He published them; or rather he made them the basis of sections of a book published in 1797. The journalist did not limit himself to telling the world about Hamilton's affair with Mrs. Reynolds. Having defamed the former treasury head, he proceeded to do the same to the three men—Muhlenberg, Venable, and Monroe—with whom Hamilton had shared his secret. Callender accused the Republican trio of knowing the real story and of deliberately suppressing it. What was the real story? According to Callender, Hamilton had not only committed adultery with Maria Reynolds, he had also conspired with her husband to line his own pockets by using public funds to speculate in government securities while Secretary of the Treasury.

In eighteenth-century America lurid books came in sober covers. The title of Callender's journalistic soap opera was *The History of the United States for the Year 1796.*

As Hamilton perused its pages, his dismay was exceeded only by his bewilderment. Who could have told the journalist about the Reynolds Affair? One of the three Republicans? He found that hard to believe. His disapproval of their political views did not extend to their characters. He regarded them as gentlemen, incapable of breaking a promise made to another gentleman.

Still the matter must be looked into. He sent the three almost identical letters. He assured them of his continued faith in their word, but added that under the circumstances he would appreciate receiving from them statements to the effect that they had not revealed his secret and that they did not endorse the ugly charges that Callender had hurled at him. Muhlenberg and Venable answered him at once, each supplying precisely the statements he had requested. But from James Monroe—nothing!

For a brief period Hamilton made excuses for Monroe's silence. No longer a Senator, the Virginia statesman had only recently returned from France after two years as the American minister there. With relations between that country and the United States in troubled and violent flux, it followed that Monroe was a busy man with much on his mind. As the weeks slipped by, however, and still no word came from the Virginian, a disquieting suspicion took form in Hamilton's mind.

From Callender's *History of the United States for the Year 1796,* he had learned something he had not previously known. In January of 1793, only a few weeks after the three Republicans had signed the memorandum declaring Hamilton innocent of dishonesty in office, Monroe had paid a second call on Jacob Clingman, Reynolds' then imprisoned partner. From Clingman the Virginian had obtained and apparently had accepted as true a written declaration that Hamilton had not told the full story of his relations with James Reynolds, that he *had* used Reynolds' services to cover up illegal speculation in government securities.

In July of 1797 Hamilton wrote Monroe again. His second letter was stronger than the first had been. This time he mentioned the secret visit Monroe had made to Reynolds' partner, and asked the Virginian to repudiate the charges that Clingman had made. "And I shall rely on your delicacy," Hamilton wrote, "that the manner of doing it will be such as one gentleman has a right to expect from another."

Hamilton's second letter, like his first one, went unanswered—a situation that converted his suspicions into convictions. The Virginian's continued silence lent itself to only one interpretation: Monroe was the man who had made possible the revelations in Callender's book. Learning that the Virginian was in New York, Hamilton called on him. Their confrontation was a stormy one. Monroe denied any responsibility for Callender's revelations and charges. As for Hamilton's demand that he publicly repudiate the accusations made, he agreed to talk that over with his political cohorts and do something about it; he did not specify just what.

What he did was confer with Jefferson and other Republicans. From them he learned that the leaders of his party still hoped to prove Hamilton guilty of peculations in office. Even now they were questioning a man who had held a small position in the treasury department during Hamilton's secretaryship. Never mind that this man had emphatically cleared his superior of all wrongdoing. The Republican chieftains remained convinced that sooner or later the evidence they were seeking would show up. Meanwhile, Monroe decided, it would be smart politics to refrain from attesting to the fiscal innocence of the "great embezzler."

Angry and desperate, Hamilton took the only course he considered open to a gentleman whose honor had been questioned. He wrote to Monroe, telling him to send a statement clearing his name or give him satisfaction in another way. In other words, Hamilton challenged the Virginian to a duel, and Monroe, in the flowery language of the Code Duello, immediately accepted.

At this point the episode took an ironic turn. For the now seemingly inevitable duel, Hamilton chose as his second an old army friend. Monroe selected Aaron Burr, and this fascinating man, whose dueling pistol would one day terminate

Alexander Hamilton's life, proceeded to play the peace-maker. He dropped a soothing word here and a gentle suggestion there. Once he even withheld from Hamilton's gaze an inflammatory letter that Monroe had written. By these and other devices, patiently applied, he persuaded the principals to the quarrel to settle it with words instead of with pistols or swords.

Burr's good work did not bring the episode to its climax. The impetuous Mr. Hamilton attended to that. He could not bring himself to leave the American people under the impression that his masterpiece—his grand financial scheme—was the work of a dishonorable man. Determined to destroy any such impression forever, he published in the autumn of 1797 a book in answer to the one Callender had written. In view of its lively contents, Hamilton's book was even less alluringly titled than Callender's had been. He called it *Observations on Certain Documents contained in No. V and VI of "The History of the United States for the Year 1796," in which the charge of speculation against Alexander Hamilton, late Secretary of the Treasury, is fully refuted. Written by himself.* Five years before, Hamilton had told three of his political foes about his illicit relations with Maria Reynolds in order to prove his financial integrity. In his *Observations on Certain Documents,* he made the same confession to the American public for the same reason.

Callender had pictured Hamilton as forcing his attentions on Mrs. Reynolds. Hamilton correctly described himself as a greenhorn who had been taken in by one of the oldest extortion rackets known to man—a painful admission, coming from a suave New Yorker who prided himself on his knowledge of the wickedness of a world where few men were estimable, fewer amiable.

In the terminology of modern times, Hamilton's book was a best seller. Even so, it failed to convince his enemies that he had conducted himself honestly while Secretary of the United States Treasury. As Thomas Jefferson shrewdly observed, the former Secretary's public admission of "one crime was not a convincing way to establish his innocence of another."

On this unsatisfactory note ended the drama that John T. Callender's contemptible book had brought into being. Callender and his silent partner, John Beckley, had played their roles with a flair that should have been bestowed on more worthy efforts. Monroe had behaved evasively, Burr gracefully, and Hamilton more boldly than wisely. But if the drama was without heroes, it did not lack for a heroine. Betsey Schuyler Hamilton never breathed so much as a word of reproach to her erring husband. She would not forget what he had done, but she forgave him promptly and magnanimously.

☆   ☆   ☆

Public interest in Hamilton's book was blissfully short-lived. At the time of its publication the American people had other and more important things to think about. Since the outbreak of the French Revolution, the frequently changing governments of that country had been a source of almost as much trouble in the New World as in the Old.

On two occasions French envoys to the United States had conducted themselves in a manner that had outraged even such apostles of neutrality as Washington and such friends of the French Revolution as Thomas Jefferson. During the closing months of Washington's administration, relations between the two countries edged toward the breaking point when, in January of 1796, the current rulers of France—a five-man executive body known as the Directory—ordered their navy to confiscate American ships carrying articles produced or manufactured in England or her possessions. By the time John Adams took over the presidency, only a little more than a year later, armed French vessels known as "picaroons" had sunk or captured almost three hundred merchantmen flying the flag of the United States.

In the late summer of 1797, Adams sped three ministers plenipotentiary to France in an effort to stop this piecemeal destruction of his country's trade. Rife among the members of the Directory at this point was the corruption that a few years later would make it easy for Napoleon Bonaparte to seize control of the French government. When the American envoys reached Paris, they were compelled for many weeks to cool their heels in the anteroom of the Directory's offices. When they finally moved from anteroom to conference room, three agents of Charles Maurice de Talleyrand, the French foreign minister, confronted them with an amazing proposition. Arrange for a huge American loan to France and pay us a bribe of two hundred and fifty thousand dollars, they said—or go home. The American envoys went home, giving rise to the legendary slogan that their countrymen would soon be echoing from one end of the United States to the other: "Millions for defense but not one cent for tribute!"

No American was more eager to see his government spending millions for defense than Hamilton. He had already called on Congress to enlarge the country's tiny army and its barely visible navy. Heretofore his pleas had fallen on deaf ears. More precisely, they had fallen on the ears of the Republicans, who were universally opposed to spending money on guns and warships and who had enough votes in

Congress to block all efforts to do so. Then in the closing weeks of 1798, President Adams published the "XYZ Papers," the correspondence covering the attempt by the agents of the French foreign minister to bribe the American envoys. Overnight, so to speak, the shocked indignation of the American people washed like a wave into the halls of Congress, where enough Republicans quickly joined with the Federalists to pass a series of measures designed to put America on a war footing. These laws increased the size of the army, authorized the construction of a fleet of warships, and established in the Cabinet a new post to be known as the Secretary of the Navy.

☆　　☆　　☆

Hamilton's thinking about these developments merits examination, if only to dispel a notion prevalent then and later that he looked upon a stronger military establishment solely as a weapon against a government he hated, the "terrible republic" as he called the French Directory. In truth, France was not the only nation he feared. Much as he admired Great Britain, he realized that in recent years she had become almost as much of a threat. To a lesser degree, her navy was also preying on American shipping, a practice it would continue until the eve of the War of 1812.

Hamilton's insistence on strengthening the armed forces rested on far more than his disapproval of revolutionary France. Behind it lay his conviction that as long as the United States remained militarily weak, it would be at the mercy of every European nation with sufficient sea power to float an invading army across the Atlantic Ocean.

This is not to say that in 1797 he did not want and fully anticipate a war with France. If at that time he refused to join the hue and cry of the many citizens calling for an immediate attack on the "terrible republic," it was only because he realized that the United States was not yet prepared.

"Hard words," he reminded the warhawks, thundering from every corner of the land, "are rarely useful in public proceedings. *Real firmness* is good for everything. *Strut* is good for nothing." It would take time, he warned, to build a three thousand five hundred-man army into a ten thousand-man army, to change a navy consisting of three unfinished frigates into an effective striking fleet. He urged the country to try to settle its differences with France by diplomacy even as it prepared for war. He took the position that, whatever happened, the United States should not strike first. Let France invade; let the onus of initiating the hostilities fall on her.

That in time she would initiate them, he was certain. Nor did the prospect displease him. Still residing within the adult Hamilton was the youth who years before had cried "I wish there was a war!" He had not forgotten his moment of glory on the battlefields of Yorktown. In the martial spirit sweeping the country in 1798 he espied, so to speak, a chance to enjoy a second Yorktown. Someone would have to command the country's new and enlarged army. Casting an eye over the surviving generals of the Revolutionary War, he came to a scarcely surprising conclusion. Save for Washington, in his opinion, none of them was as well qualified as himself.

Washington's departure from the presidency had not diminished the New Yorker's influence on national affairs to the extent he had once feared it would. The second President had inherited his Cabinet from the first. Practically all of its members were devoted to the one-time treasury head.

Hamilton had only to mention his wish to one of these gentlemen—Timothy Pickering, the Secretary of State. He
could count on Pickering to take the next step.

Pickering took it a few days later as he and Adams sat
chatting in a parlor of the presidential mansion in Philadelphia. "Mr. Secretary," said the President, "whom shall
we appoint Commander-in-Chief?" Pickering's reply was
prompt and eager. "Colonel Hamilton," he said. In the
words of one of Hamilton's biographers, the President
"could hardly have been more startled had a snake crawled
from under the sofa." His agitated shake of the leonine
Adams head put the heavy Adams jowls into motion. "Oh
no!" he exclaimed, "it is not his turn by a great deal. I
would sooner appoint . . . ," and the President rattled off
the names of several Revolutionary officers. When Pickering
argued that none of them had Hamilton's "transcendent
ability," Adams cut short the conversation with the statement that "in these critical times" he had no intention of
entrusting the Army of the United States to that "Creole,"
one of his kinder appellations for Alexander Hamilton.

Determined to keep the "Creole" out of the commander-
ship, Adams shortly did the one thing he was certain would
accomplish that end. He sent a letter to Mount Vernon, im-
ploring its aging master to help his beleaguered country by
once more leading its armies as commander-in-chief. Washington replied that he had no desire for an important post
ever again. In view of the troubles besetting the Republic,
however, he agreed to take the post under two conditions.

One was that he be allowed to remain on inactive duty
until such time as actual hostilities with France broke out.
The other was that his second in command be Alexander
Hamilton.

On this letter President Adams bent a round and stricken

eye. Obviously he was hoist on his own petard. He could not tell the Father of His Country to throw his conditions into the Potomac River. He could only accept Washington's offer on Washington's terms—an action that had the effect of making Alexander Hamilton the actual commander of the American forces with the rank of major general and the title of inspector general.

Making his headquarters in Philadelphia, Hamilton spent the next two years pulling the country's new army into shape. They were busy years but, from his point of view, less than satisfactory ones. His only battle was with John Adams. He had won the opening skirmish of that, but the battle itself went to the doughty New Englander.

Shortly after the XYZ Affair, the President had announced that he would send no more envoys to France until he was certain the French Directory would receive them with dignity. Then in 1799, in a move that caught not only Hamilton but the whole country by surprise, Adams dispatched a second peace mission to Paris.

During the intervening months internal tensions had chastened the members of the corrupt French Directory. This time the American ministers encountered no attempt at bribery, no insults. Instead they wrung from the French rulers what amounted to an agreement to desist from preying on American shipping.

In this manner, toward the end of John Adams' administration, America's undeclared war with France arrived at its happy ending. With the war scare gone, Adams ordered the army reduced to its former size, and Inspector General Hamilton put aside his dreams of further military glory and returned to his law office in New York.

☆   ☆   ☆

The verdict of time is that, in sending a mission to France in October of 1799, John Adams performed "an act of rare courage and statesmanship." Politically, it was also an act of self-sacrifice; it as good as guaranteed that he would not be elected to the presidency a second time.

Never was a peace more unpopular. The warhawks, and there were many of them, had their hearts set on a scrap with the "terrible republic." They were furious when Adams denied them the privilege. One is tempted to suggest that the seeds of the War of 1812 were planted at this point. Cheated of one war by a wise and far-seeing President, the American people only a dozen years later would go lunging into another war that could have been just as easily and as honorably averted.

Adams' despised peace was not the only obstacle confronting the Federalists as in 1800 the fourth presidential election got underway. During his administration, Congress had passed and the President had signed the Alien and Sedition Acts. These attempts to limit free speech and to make life difficult for immigrants not yet naturalized would look worse to future Americans than they did to those who saw them in force. To be sure, in the South and in New York Republican strategists drummed up supporters by denouncing the acts. Most Americans, however, were not much touched by them.

What did touch them was the money the country had spent on Inspector General Hamilton's big army. Some citizens were for the peace, but all were against the added taxes required to support an army raised for a war that had blown up in their faces.

In the summer the party caucuses chose their candidates. Again the Republican nominees were Jefferson and Burr. Again the Federalists selected Adams, although his companion on the ticket was Charles Cotesworth Pinckney of South Carolina, brother of the Thomas Pinckney who had occupied that position four years before.

As if the Federalists did not have enough troubles, Hamilton now presented them with more. Instead of concentrating his fire on the opposition nominees, Jefferson and Burr, he wrote and had printed a stinging attack on the President entitled "Letter from Alexander Hamilton concerning the Public Conduct and Character of John Adams."

We can only speculate on the motives that drove the inspector general's hand as he penned this philippic. Washington had died during the preceding year; and it has been plausibly suggested that his death removed from the scene the one man capable of restraining Alexander Hamilton from expressing a seemingly irresistible bent toward self-destruction.

Hamilton's plan was to circulate his anti-Adams pamphlet only among carefully selected Federalists. But in New York that wily Republican tactician, Aaron Burr, was keeping a close eye on developments. Somehow Burr learned about the pamphlet, and somehow he obtained a copy of it. One can all but hear his gleeful chuckles as he delivered Hamilton's strictures on Adams to the press to be published for public consumption—thus placing before the American people the spectacle of a ranking Federalist in the act of condemning the presidential candidate of his own party. Hamilton had written more than a philippic; he had written an epitaph, reading in effect: "Here lies the Federalist Party, done to death by the pen of its most brilliant spokesman."

In the popular election in November the Federalists went down to a defeat from which they would never recover. Their leaders, however, had no monopoly on political ineptitude.

The Republican leaders made their own blunders. Their intent was to put Jefferson in the presidency, but by a series of clumsy manipulations they came close to defeating their own ends. The balloting in the Electoral College resulted in a tie. Jefferson and Burr got seventy-three votes apiece, a development that threw the election into the House of Representatives where in February of 1801, when the voting began there, the Federalists were still in the majority.

When the House of Representatives selects the chief executive, the unit rule prevails: each state, irrespective of the size of its delegation, can cast only one vote. A majority is required to elect. Under the Constitution as it stood in 1801 this meant that to become President one of the candidates, Jefferson or Burr, had to receive the votes of nine of the then sixteen states—at which point the other man would be automatically elected to the vice presidency.

Long before the members of the House began balloting in a small and airless room of the recently occupied Capitol building in Washington, Hamilton had made up his mind. "Jefferson or Burr?" he said crisply, echoing a question put to him by a close friend. "Jefferson, of course!"

His decision reflected no change of heart or mind about "the great demagogue from Virginia." It merely reflected his even more intense disapproval of Aaron Burr. Wrongheaded though Jefferson was, Hamilton observed, he at least had principles. Burr, in his opinion, had none. Hamilton called the dapper Republican leader "the most unfit and dangerous man in the community," a man who despised the people but pandered to their wishes to further his own ends. "In short," the inspector general declared, "if we have an embryo Caesar in the United States, 'tis Burr."

As the House election drew near, a stream of letters went from Hamilton to prominent Federalists both in and out of

Congress. On the whole the responses of those on the outside were favorable. They agreed with the inspector general that Jefferson was the lesser of the two Republican evils. In the House of Representatives, however, among the men who now really counted, the response was just the opposite. Almost to a man, the Federalist Congressmen were convinced that behind Aaron Burr's democratic façade beat the heart of a true gentleman, which was to say of a Federalist. Caucusing on the eve of the voting, they bound themselves to follow the dictates of their leaders in the House. Those dictates were "Vote for Burr."

Vote for him they did. The House election was no sooner in train on the morning of February 11 than it was plain that the tie vote in the Electoral College had plunged the country into its gravest crisis since the battle over ratifying the Constitution. For seven raucous days and six sleepless nights the voting continued. Thirty-five times the roll was called, and every time the results were the same: eight states for Jefferson, six for Burr, and two divided.*

With the end of Adams' term only a few weeks away, rumors and alarums coursed the country. Republicans saw a conspiracy by their enemies to prolong the House election

---

* A word of explanation: The House of Representatives in February of 1801 had 106 members. Fifty-five were Federalists, giving their party a clear majority. Even so, under the unit rule they were at a disadvantage. The geographical distribution in the House was such that the Federalists controlled only six states whereas the Republicans controlled eight. As for the remaining states, Maryland and Vermont, their delegations were evenly split. Consistently throughout the first thirty-five roll calls of the House presidential election, Maryland's four Federalists voted for Burr and her four Republicans for Jefferson. Similarly, Vermont's one Federalist voted for Burr and her one Republican for Jefferson. Consequently, the vote was always the same: eight states for Jefferson, six for Burr, two divided.

beyond inauguration day in an attempt to keep the government in Federalist hands. Prophets of woe were everywhere, forecasting disunion, the downfall of the Constitution, and worse.

Who could break the deadlock? Not Hamilton. His influence no longer reached into the halls of Congress. Credit for resolving the crisis goes to stalwart James Asheton Bayard of Delaware and five other Federalist Congressmen wise and brave enough to put nation above party.

Bayard was the principal figure among them. His was a strong position. As the only representative from his state, he could end the election at any point simply by changing his vote from Burr to Jefferson. This he did not do. His ability to do so, however, gave his arguments force when he pointed out to his fellow Federalists that for them to prolong the deadlock was, in his words, "to risk the Constitution and civil war." Reluctantly they bowed to his good sense, and the deed was done.

It was done in such a manner that no Federalist had to vote for Jefferson. As a matter of fact, one Federalist—Benjamin Huger of South Carolina—had been voting for him all along. On the thirty-sixth ballot, however, Huger agreed to withhold his vote, and his four Federalist colleagues did the same, so that South Carolina voted blank, meaning that it registered no vote at all. As the lone delegate from Delaware, Bayard followed the same procedure, his state's vote also a blank. The election was decided in the Maryland and Vermont delegations. The four Maryland Federalists refrained from voting; this action, since their colleagues were Republicans, put their state in the Jefferson column. By withholding his vote, the Vermont Federalist permitted his Republican colleague to throw that state to Jefferson. Result, announced to an anxious citizenry on February 17: ten states for Jefferson, making him President-elect; four for Burr, giving him the vice presidency; and two blanks.

☆   ☆   ☆

To Hamilton it was a relief to see the "embryo Caesar" denied the presidency, but as he watched the progress of the Jefferson administration, he saw in it precisely what he had expected to see—a drift toward democracy that he was certain would lead the Republic into disorder and anarchy. Some of his Federalist associates, a group known as the Essex Junto, expressed their disgust by calling for secession. They advocated setting up in New England and New York a separate nation, insulated against the horrors they discerned in the growing power of the people.

Hamilton held aloof from this movement. He did not think the country could be saved by making two countries of it. As he put it, the "poison of Democracy" had permeated the nation's veins; subdividing it, he said, would only spread the "disease."

In 1800 he purchased thirty acres in what was then rural Manhattan, now a heavily populated section north of City College. There he built a fine square house with many fireplaces and a low balustrade surmounting the cornice. He called it the Grange, after the ancestral seat of his father's family in Scotland. Moving to the Grange in 1801, he set about living the life of a country gentleman. In a plaintive letter to a friend he explained the significance of this change. "A disappointed politician you know," he wrote, "is very apt to take refuge in a garden."

Letters to other friends during this period of his life were redolent with his despondency over the direction the country was taking. A man dissatisfied with the present tends to think on the past. As the nineteenth century began, Hamilton brooded much on earlier and happier days. He recalled often how at Poughkeepsie he had single-handedly persuaded anti-Federalist New York to ratify the Constitution. Even then he had feared that the document framed by the Founding Fathers did not provide the strong central government by the few for the many that he felt the Republic must have. To his friend, Gouverneur Morris, he wrote:

Mine is an odd destiny; perhaps no man in the United States has sacrificed or done more for the present Constitution than myself; and contrary to all my anticipations of its fate, as you know from the very beginning, I am still laboring to prop the frail and worthless fabric, yet I have the murmurs of its friends no less than the curses of its foes for my reward. What can I do better than withdraw from the scene? Every day proves to me more and more that this American world was not made for me.

If the early months of 1801 were bleak to him, those that followed were worse. By the summer of that year his family had grown to seven children with the eighth and last one on the way.

His favorite was his oldest son, Philip. At age twenty, Philip was a bright and handsome young man. Friends of the family differed as to his qualities. To one of them he was "a sad rake," plainly headed for terrible disgrace. To another he was a "chip off the old block," bound in time to become as great a man as his father.

Whatever Philip's potentialities, he was not to realize

them. On Independence Day, George Eacker, a young New York lawyer described in the Federalist press as "a violent and bitter democrat," delivered an harangue loaded with remarks derogatory to Philip's father. Chancing to meet Eacker at the theater, Philip challenged him to a duel, and the young lawyer accepted. A few days later they faced one another on a woodsy ledge above the Hudson River on the outskirts of the New Jersey village of Weehawken.

Unknown to Eacker, Philip had decided to withhold his first shot. It is not clear whether he did this to show his contempt for Eacker or his disapproval of dueling. In any event, Eacker's first ball caught him in the chest, and Philip's pistol fired accidentally as he fell—a chain of events similar to those that would occur in this same sylvan glade only three years later. His friends carried the wounded youth to the Grange. There, during the night, he died in his father's arms.

Hamilton had to call on all his strength to surmount this loss. His wife took even longer to get over it, and Angelica, their oldest daughter, never did. A beautiful girl who had inherited her father's musical talent, Angelica had doted on her older brother. Soon after his death her mind snapped. Although she lived to the age of seventy-three, she never recovered.

The Reynolds Affair and its disclosure to the leering eyes of the world—Philip's death—Angelica's insanity: truly Alexander Hamilton and his family had suffered much. And just around the corner of their lives a still more poignant tragedy lay in wait.

10

Interview in Weehawken

During Alexander Hamilton's occupancy of the treasury office, there sat in the United States Senate a hard-bitten farmer from the backwoods of Pennsylvania named William Maclay. Senator Maclay was a Jeffersonian long before Thomas Jefferson was generally recognized as the fountainhead of American democracy. During the Pennsylvanian's senatorial career, he kept a diary into which he poured his opinions of the governmental figures around him.

Maclay was a specialist in human weakness. No sooner did his gaze alight on a public idol than it traveled at once and unerringly to that part of the idol's anatomy known as "clay feet." To the sharp-eyed diarist President Washington was a mountain of gloomy mediocrity. He wrote of Washington's Vice President, "Bonny Johnny Adams," that he was forever "mantling his visage with the most unmeaning simper that ever dimpled the face of folly."

As for Washington's first treasury head—for that bastion of conservatism the liberal Senator from Pennsylvania reserved the unkindest cut of all. Coming away from his first actual meeting with the then Secretary, Maclay concluded that the United States had placed its delicate financial problems in the hands of a "giddy" boy.

Many people, knowing Hamilton only in passing, got this impression of him. In social gatherings his lips gushed small talk. He was a master of what was known in the drawing rooms of his day as the *bon mot*, the memorable play-on-words, the rapier-swift joke. He was always ready, in a convivial gathering of men only, to lift his glass and render a lusty ballad in his rich singing voice. His smile came easily; his laugh lay close to the surface.

As we have had occasion to observe, however, behind this lightsome exterior lay a penetrating and profoundly sober mind. It was a mind, moreover, characterized by a tendency to melancholy that in the closing years of his life sometimes bordered on morbidity. The twentieth-century reader can scarcely fail to note the spiritual resemblance between Alexander Hamilton and France's Charles de Gaulle. Nor is he likely to overlook the similarity of Hamilton's preoccupations to those of Shakepeare's Prince of Denmark, dolorously pondering "whether 'tis nobler in the mind to suffer the slings and arrows of outrageous fortune, Or to take arms against a sea of troubles, and by opposing, end them."

We must assume that Hamilton's fateful quarrel with Aaron Burr incubated in the shadows of that Hamlet-like mind. It cannot be explained by reference to politics alone. In that arena the two men had battled one another for fifteen years. More often than not, Burr had been the winner; but if Hamilton had dueled with everyone who triumphed over him in this respect, he would have had time for little else.

Only nominally was Burr a Republican. Actually he was an independent whose close and devoted followers, the so-called Burrites, constituted a sort of party within a party and provided their leader with a power base that other political leaders, Federalist and Republican alike, viewed with ill-concealed envy. Hamilton admired George Washington's refusal to align himself officially with any political group; but in his eyes, what was a virtue in the great Virginian was a vice in his fellow New Yorker, whose inclination to see some good on both sides of the political fence struck Hamilton as the attitude of a man devoid of principle.

Burr was famous for his courteous treatment of everyone, rich or poor, important or obscure. To his followers, the Burrites, this was his most engaging quality. To Hamilton it was proof positive, as he repeatedly asserted, that the handsome attorney-politician was a power-hungry opportunist engaged in ingratiating himself with the people in order to dominate them.

How good or bad a man Aaron Burr really was is a question that may never be answered to the satisfaction of everyone. The point to be stressed here is that in the eyes of Alexander Hamilton, he was "the most profligate man in the country." As early as 1792, when Burr had the effrontery to defeat Hamilton's father-in-law in a race for the United States Senate, Hamilton began making his feelings on this point crystal clear to personal friends and political cronies.

In letter after letter he likened Burr to Catiline, the Roman patrician who, during the century preceding the birth of Christ, tried unsuccessfully to overthrow the government and seize power. In sections of his correspondence Hamilton carried his criticisms beyond the limits commonly regarded as allowable to political adversaries. Occasionally he alluded to Burr's private life, describing it as "impure." He pointed out, accurately enough, that the dressy New York attorney consistently lived beyond his means and was deeply in debt. Burr, he insisted in a letter typical of many others, was "deficient in honesty. . . . As a politician . . . he has but one principle—to *get power* by *any* means and to *keep* it by *all* means."

In New York the two rivals moved in the same social and legal circles. They knew the same people. As Burr would later confide to his friend Charles Biddle, a Philadelphia merchant, he was aware for several years of the fierceness and frequency of Hamilton's attacks on him. So long as these appeared only in private correspondence, however, he could do nothing about them.

Then in April of 1804 an Albany newspaper published an account of a local dinner party at which Hamilton was heard to declare "in substance . . . that he looked upon Mr. Burr to be a dangerous man." To this the author of these revelations added that he himself "could detail . . . a still more despicable opinion which General Hamilton has expressed of Mr. Burr."

As a gentleman and a subscriber to the Code Duello, Burr could not ignore this public assault on his honor even if he had wanted to—and there is plentiful evidence that he did not want to. His eyes did not actually fall on the offending newspaper story until almost three months after its publication. Although in the interval no one seems to have paid much attention to the article, Burr acted on it at once—a circumstance which suggests that he saw in the situation a long-awaited opportunity to force Hamilton to either prove or withdraw what Burr described as "numberless depredations on my fame and character."

For more than a week, beginning on June 18, a string of communications, some written and some oral, passed between the two men. Young William P. Van Ness acted as Burr's messenger and second. Nathaniel Pendleton performed these chores for Hamilton. Accompanied by a clipping of the Albany newspaper article, Burr's opening message was brief and testy. He called on his rival to either acknowledge or disavow "the still more despicable opinion" of himself that the article attributed to Hamilton.

The tone of Burr's note struck Hamilton as "menacing," all the more so because it was delivered by Van Ness, who on several occasions had served as Burr's second in duels. Convinced that his rival was not interested in an apology, but was only leading up to what Van Ness called a "personal interview"—a duel, Hamilton sent back a longer but equally testy message. He pointed out that Burr was asking the impossible. How could he either acknowledge or deny a "still more despicable opinion" without knowing what it was? If Burr would specify the precise "opinion," he would be happy to do something about it.

Burr considered this answer evasive and insulting. He was particularly incensed to find in Hamilton's letter a dissertation on the meaning of the word "despicable." To Burr that word, as used in the newspaper article, meant only one thing. Obviously Hamilton had said something about his private life or his personal character that even a politician had no right to say about another politician. In subsequent messages he demanded that Hamilton deny having ever said anything slanderous about him in public or in private.

No doubt the dispute would have closed at this point, had Hamilton acceded to his rival's demand. An honest man, fully conscious that over the years he had figuratively torn Aaron Burr's reputation to shreds, Hamilton could not bring himself to do this. On July 3 his opponent challenged, and he accepted with a request, promptly granted, that the actual "interview" be postponed until the eleventh to permit him to wind up pressing legal business.

During the interval, Hamilton drew up his will and wrote several letters to be opened by his wife and others in the event of his death. Among these was the remarkable document recording his decision to withhold his fire, at least during the opening rounds of the impending duel. It was a pious youth who three decades before had sailed from the West Indies to complete his education in colonial America. During the intervening years he had shown, on the whole, only a formal interest in religion. Of late, however, and especially since the death of his son, the old fervor had returned. "My religious and moral principles," he wrote on or about July 4:

> are strongly opposed to the practice of Duelling, and it would ever give me pain to be obliged to shed the blood of a fellow creature in a private combat forbidden by the laws.

> As well because it is possible that I may have injured Col. Burr, however convinced myself that my opinions and declarations have been well founded, as from my general principles and temper in relation to similar affairs—I have resolved . . . to *reserve* and *throw away*

my first fire, and I *have thoughts* even of reserving my
second fire—and thus giving a double opportunity to
Col. Burr to pause and to reflect.

A heaviness in the air promised a warm day when, shortly
after five o'clock on the morning of July 11, 1804, Hamilton
left his country home to keep his appointment with Aaron
Burr. His destination was the same Field of Honor in Weehawken where three years earlier his son Philip had fallen,
mortally wounded. The State of New York had severe laws
against dueling, and this grassy ledge on the Jersey shores of
the Hudson had long been popular with New York gentlemen determined to settle their differences with deadly
weapons.

The English-made pistols in Hamilton's case, each having
a barrel "nine inches long and of admirable workmanship,"
were the same ones that Philip had used; and before Philip,
Hamilton's brother-in-law, John Barker Church, had used
them in a duel with Aaron Burr. With Hamilton, in the
boat that carried him across the river, were Nathaniel Pendleton, his second, Dr. David Hosack, a New York physician,
and the bargeman hired to row them over.

By prearrangement, Burr and his second, Van Ness, were
already on the dueling ground when Hamilton and his party
arrived. It was a pretty place, rather like a stage setting, according to a contemporary engraving. A man standing in the
center of the area, facing the Hudson, had before him the
tops of the trees flanking "the steep and dangerous path"
leading up from the river below. Over to his right grew a
gnarled old cedar, its stiffish branches placing a lattice-like
roof over almost the entire ledge. On the other side stood a
large boulder, worn smooth by time and weather.

At approximately seven o'clock, Van Ness and Pendleton initiated the formalities required by the Code Duello—that practice, so strange to modern sensibilities, that some authorities date back at least to the encounter between David and Goliath. The two seconds stepped off the paces, marked the positions, and inspected the pistols in each other's presence. Next they cast lots to determine where the principals should stand, and by which of the seconds the command to fire should be given. In both of these tosses Pendleton, Hamilton's second, was the winner.

It is important to point out that at this time Aaron Burr had no inkling of Hamilton's intent to withhold his first shot and perhaps even his second. Certainly Hamilton's actions during these preliminaries were those of a man who, like Burr, had come to this picturesque spot to shoot and be shot at.

Once the two principals had taken their assigned positions —Hamilton near the boulder and Burr near the tree—and had cocked their pistols, Pendleton put the usual question: Were the gentlemen ready?

"Stop," said Hamilton before his second could give the command to fire. "In certain states of the light one requires glasses."

He then leveled his gun first in one direction and then in another, trying the light. Then he put on his spectacles, and repeated the experiment. Finally he informed his second that he was ready.

"Present!" said Pendleton, and the duel began.

It was over less than a second later. Burr's first shot struck Hamilton in the abdomen. As the wounded man fell, his pistol went off, apparently by accident—even as on this same greensward in 1801 his son's gun had gone off seemingly by accident as he fell.

Hamilton had not meant to shoot. Nor was he immediately aware of having done so. "Take care of that pistol," he gasped as his second rushed to his side, "it is undischarged and still cocked; it may go off and do harm. Pendleton knows that I did not intend to fire at him."

Seeing his adversary down, Burr started toward him, only to be seized by his second and literally dragged from the scene lest he be observed in the area by individuals who might later have to testify in court. The victor, it would seem, was as dazed by what had happened as his victim. "I must go and speak to him," Burr kept muttering to himself as Van Ness pushed him into their waiting boat and ordered the bargeman to pull for New York.

The scene on the ledge behind them was an agitated one. "This is a mortal wound, Doctor," Hamilton said to Hosack as the physician bent to examine him. Then he fell into a coma, only to revive somewhat shortly after the doctor and Pendleton had placed him in the boat and the oarsman had shoved off.

Putting in at one of the Manhattan wharfs, they carried the dying man to the home of a mutual friend, William Bayard, on what is now Jane Street in the Greenwich Village section of the city. Even before reaching the shore, Hamilton had instructed his companions to summon his wife. "Let the event be gradually broken to her," he said, "but give her hopes."

They did their best. When Betsey arrived, the seven children with her, they told her that her husband was suffering from "spasms." She did not believe them, sensing at once that he had fallen, like his son before him, in a duel. Only Hamilton could quiet her. *"Remember, my Eliza, you are Christian,"* he told her in a whisper that somehow calmed her.

Burr's bullet had penetrated his liver, lodging in the vertebrae. Hosack called in the surgeons from a French frigate then in the New York harbor. They confirmed his diagnosis and called the case hopeless. Hamilton's sufferings were intense. Even laudanum, lavishly administered, had little effect, although toward the end the pains mercifully diminished.

As death approached, he expressed a desire to be received into the Episcopal Church and to receive the sacrament. So strong was the feeling against dueling in the city that a number of clergymen approached by his friends refused to grant his request. Finally Benjamin Moore, the second Protestant Episcopal bishop of New York and president of Columbia College, consented to do so—and a few hours later, at two o'clock on the afternoon of July 12, 1804, Alexander Hamilton died.

☆   ☆   ☆

The uproar that surged across the country at news of the tragedy was shot through with stunned horror at the untimely passing of a great statesman. As for Aaron Burr, when both New Jersey and his own state indicted him for murder —New York gratuitously since it had no jurisdiction over the act—he hid out temporarily, first with his friend Charles Biddle in Philadelphia and then in the South. After which he returned to Washington to complete his term as Vice President of the United States, confident that eventually the indictments against him would be dropped, as indeed they were. Later he provided the country with another *cause célèbre* when his mysterious venture into the Southwest brought him before a Federal court jury that reluctantly acquitted him of a charge of treason in one of history's most sensational trials.

Burr was not a complainer, but the noisy indignation over the Interview in Weehawken moved him to some bitter observations. To Charles Biddle he voiced his belief that much of the outcry was motivated not by love of Hamilton but by "malice" toward himself.

There was a good deal of truth in Burr's remark. Some Federalist leaders saw in the public's anger at the New York Republican the possibility of a revival of the power that they had lost, irrevocably as it turned out, during the last presidential election. Many Republican leaders were glad to see the maverick chieftain of the Burrites laid low.

On the other hand, among the common people there was a genuine feeling of loss. Even in his heyday, Hamilton had never been a wholly popular figure. Instinctively the generality of Americans had pulled away from a man whose aristocratic ideas were at odds with their determination to build in the New World a society free of the restrictions on human liberty that their ancestors had endured in the Old World.

Now that the "Colossus of Monocrats" was dead, however, the people forgot his views and remembered the man. They remembered that, whatever his views, he had always stated them fully and openly. He had never trimmed. He had never compromised his principles in the interests of his own personal advancement. Even the Republicans—the Democrats, as people were starting to call them—conceded at last that the "great embezzler" had stolen nothing from his country and had given it much.

He certainly had. The value of his grand financial scheme to an infant Republic cannot possibly be overstated. Many years after his death, his widow, in her inimitable manner, summed up his contribution.

"Never forget," she said to a distinguished caller in her home, an American historian famous for his Jeffersonian

leanings, "that my husband *made* your government."
Exaggerated? Not much. The American people have
every reason to remember Alexander Hamilton with gratitude and affection.

Bibliography

The following list includes only those books and articles that I have found especially useful in the preparation of this book. In addition—with the kind permission of the institutions mentioned—I have made considerable use of the manuscripts of Alexander Hamilton, Thomas Jefferson, and Aaron Burr in the Library of Congress, the National Archives, the New York Historical Society, the Historical Society of Pennsylvania, the American Philosophical Society, the Massachusetts Historical Society, the Columbia University libraries, the library of Princeton University, and the library of Yale University.

Adams, James Truslow. *The Living Jefferson.* New York, 1941.

Alden, John Richard. *The American Revolution 1775–1783.* New York, 1954.

Boyd, George Adams. *Elias Boudinot: Patriot and Statesman.* Princeton, N.J., 1952.

Boyd, Julian P. *Number 7, Alexander Hamilton's Secret Attempts to Control American Foreign Policy, with Supporting Documents.* Princeton, N.J., 1964.

Burdon, Katharine Janet. *A Handbook of St. Kitts-Nevis.* London, 1920.

Dewey, Davis Rich. *Financial History of the United States,* 10th ed. New York, 1928.

Donnan, Elizabeth, ed. "Papers of James A. Bayard 1796–1815." *Annual Report of the American Historical Association for the Year 1913.* Vol. II. Washington, 1915.

Edwards, Bryan. *The History of the British West Indies.* 5th ed. Vol. I. London, 1819.

Freeman, Douglas Southall. *George Washington, A Biography.* Vols. IV (1951) and V (1952). New York.

Hamilton, Alexander. *The Papers of.* . . . Harold C. Syrett, ed.; Jacob E. Cooke, assoc. ed. New York, 1961—.

Hamilton, Allan McLane. *The Intimate Life of Alexander Hamilton.* New York, 1910.

Jefferson, Thomas. *The Papers of.* . . . Julian P. Boyd, ed. Princeton, N.J., 1950—.

Koch, Adrienne. *Jefferson and Madison: The Great Collaboration.* New York, 1950.

Larson, Harold. "Alexander Hamilton—the Fact and Fiction of His Early Years." *William & Mary Quarterly,* 3d Ser., IX (April 1952), pp. 141–151.

Maclay, Edgar, ed. *The Journal of William Maclay.* New York, 1927.

Marsh, Philip M. "John Beckley, Mystery Man of the Early

Jeffersonians." *Pennsylvania Magazine of History and Biography.* Vol. 72 (January 1948), pp. 54–69.

Miller, John C. *Alexander Hamilton, Portrait in Paradox.* New York, 1959.

Miller, Samuel. *Memoirs of the Rev. John Rodger, D.D.* New York, 1813.

Miner, Clarence Eugene. "The Ratification of the Federal Constitution by the State of New York." *Studies in History, Economics and Public Law.* Vol. 94, No. 3, pp. 379–500. New York, 1921.

Mitchell, Broadus. *Alexander Hamilton, Youth to Maturity.* New York, 1957.

————. *Alexander Hamilton: The National Adventure 1788–1804.* New York, 1962.

————. "The Man Who Discovered Hamilton." *Proceedings of the New Jersey Historical Society.* Vol. LXIX, No. 2 (April 1951), pp. 88–114.

Montross, Lynn. *The Story of the Continental Army 1775–1783* (formerly *Rag, Tag and Bobtail*). New York, 1967.

Oberholtzer, E. P. *Robert Morris.* New York, 1903.

O'Brien, Michael Joseph. *Hercules Mulligan: Confidential Correspondent of General Washington.* New York, 1937.

Platt, Edmund. *The Eagle's History of Poughkeepsie. . . .* Poughkeepsie, N.Y., 1905.

Pomerantz, Sidney I. *New York, An American City, 1783–1803.* 2d. ed. Port Washington, N.Y., 1965.

Pomeroy, Mary. *The Island of Nevis: The Birthplace of Alexander Hamilton* (pamphlet). 1956.

Roddy, Edward G. "Maryland and the Presidential Election

of 1800." *Maryland Historical Magazine.* Vol. 56 (September 1961), pp. 244–268.

Simms, J. R. "Recollections of a Visit to the Weehawken Dueling Ground." *Historical Magazine.* Vol. X, Sup. 2 (1866), pp. 45–46.

Spaulding, E. Wilder. *His Excellency, George Clinton.* New York, 1938.

Steiner, Bernard C. *The Life and Correspondence of James McHenry.* Cleveland, 1907.

Stokes, I. N. Phelps. *The Iconography of Manhattan Island.* 6 vols. New York, 1928.

Syrett, Harold C., and Jean G. Cooke, eds. *Interview in Weehawken.* Middletown, Conn., 1960.

Tuckerman, Bayard. *Life of General Philip Schuyler, 1733–1804.* New York, 1903.

Whiteley, Mrs. Emily Stone. *Washington and His Aides-de-Camp.* New York, 1936.

Index

Adams, John, 31, 47, 50, 138–41, 148–54, 156, 161
Adams, John Quincy, 141
Albany, 53–4, 64–6, 79, 82–3, 95, 164–5
André, John, 72–4
Annapolis, 87–8
Arnold, Benedict, 72
Atherton, Gertrude, 4

Barber, Francis, 22
Battery, 17, 37–8
Bayard, James Asheton, 157
Bayard, William, 169
Bayard's Hill, 41–2
Beckley, John James, 142, 147
Beckman and Cruger, 7
Beckwith, George, 117
Biddle, Charles, 164, 170–1
Bloomingdale, 18
Boston, 13, 15–8, 24–5, 31–2, 37, 40–1, 51
Boudinot, Elias, 20–1
Brandywine, 50
Brooklyn, 41
Bunker Hill, 40
Burgoyne, John, 49, 52–4, 59

Burr, Aaron, 11, 22, 42, 83, 134–5, 139, 145–7, 153–8, 162–71
Burr, Aaron Sr., 11

Callender, James T., 142–7
Cambridge, 41
Canada, 49, 52, 83
Charlestown, 4–6
Chesapeake Bay, 49, 76
Chelsea, 18, 42
Christiansted, 6, 7, 9–11
Church, Angelica, 135–6
Church, John Barker, 136, 167
Clingman, Jacob, 128–9, 142, 144
Clinton, George, 89, 90, 93–8
Clinton, Henry, 47, 54–5, 58–60, 74
Connecticut, 29, 54, 72, 84, 130
Cooper, Miles, 36
Copenhagen, 9
Cornwallis, Charles, 76–8
Cruger, Nicholas, 7–10, 13–4, 16

Delaware, 87, 157
Delaware River, 10, 18, 52, 55
DePeyster's Point, 75
Dutchess County, 95–6

Eacker, George, 160

East River, 17, 41–2
Edinburgh, 29
Elizabethtown, 18–22, 26, 47
Elizabethtown Academy, 18, 21–2, 24
England, 9, 15–6, 22, 24–8, 30, 32–4, 57–60, 71, 83, 85–7, 117–8, 142, 148
Estaing, Count d', 60–1
Eton, 142

Fenno, John, 118–20
Ford, Theodosia, 62
Fort George, 17
Fort Ticonderoga, 40
France, 46, 57–8, 60, 72, 74, 103, 109–10, 117, 144, 147–53
Franklin, Benjamin, 56
Freehold, 58
Freneau, Philip, 119–20

Gates, Horatio, 52–4, 65
George III, 16, 24, 34, 41, 43, 51
Georgia, 60, 62
Georgetown, 109
Germantown, 51
Gerry, Elbridge, 94
Giles, William B., 126–7
Grange, 4, 158, 160
Greene, Nathanael, 43
Greenwich Village, 18, 169

Hamilton, Alexander (Laird of Cambuskieth), 4
Hamilton, Angelica, 160
Hamilton, Elizabeth Schuyler, 64–7, 75, 78–9, 115, 127, 132, 135–6, 147, 160, 166, 169, 171
Hamilton, James (father) of Alexander), 3, 4, 6, 7, 12–3

Hamilton, James (son of Alexander), 136
Hamilton, James Jr. (brother of Alexander), 4, 6, 7, 9
Hamilton, Philip, 78–9, 159–60, 166–7, 169
Hancock, John, 50
Harlem, 18, 42–3
Harrison, Robert Hanson, 48
Hartford, 72
Hobbes, Thomas, 35–6
Holland, 103
Hosack, David, 167, 169–70
Howe, William, 41, 43, 49, 51–2, 55, 58
Hudson River, 17, 23, 41–3, 49, 60, 64, 72, 75, 93, 95, 160, 166
Huger, Benjamin, 157

Jay, John, 31, 36–7, 93, 99, 118
Jefferson, Thomas, 33–5, 37, 61, 69, 109–21, 126, 139, 141–2, 145, 147, 153–8, 161

Kent, James, 95–6, 100
King's College (Columbia), 9, 22–3, 27, 36, 170
Kip's Bay, 42
Knox, Henry, 123–4
Knox, Hugh, 10–3, 15–6, 18, 20–2, 33
Kortright and Cruger, 7, 14, 18–9

Lafayette, Marquis de, 74, 77
Lancaster, 51
Laurens, John, 47–8, 61–2, 64, 66
Lavien, John Michael, 4
Lavien, Rachel Fawcett, 3, 4, 6–9
Lee, Charles, 58–9
Lee, Richard Henry, 50
Lexington, 37, 40

Livingston, Brockholst, 83
Livingston, Edward, 83
Livingston, William, 20–2
Locke, John, 35–6
Long Island, 41

Maclay, William, 161–2
Madison, James, 87–8, 93–4, 98–9, 113, 116
Maryland, 48, 87, 109, 156n, 157
Mason, George, 94
Massachusetts, 37, 41, 50, 85, 88, 94, 138–40
McHenry, James, 48
Middlebrook, 60
Miller, John C., 7
Monmouth, 58–9
Monroe, James, 128–30, 132–3, 141–7
Moore, Benjamin, 170
Morris, Gouverneur, 158
Morris, Robert, 71–2, 81–2, 102
Morristown, 44, 62, 66, 70–1
Mount Vernon, 135, 151
Muhlenberg, Frederick, 128–30, 141, 143–4
Mulligan, Hercules, 19, 22–3, 26, 37–40, 49

Napoleon, 120, 148
Nevis, 3–5, 11
Newark, 61
New Bridge, 72
New Brunswick, 43
New Hampshire, 96–7
New Jersey, 18–20, 22, 26, 43–4, 51, 58–9, 72, 84, 87, 160, 170
New Windsor, 73–5
New York, 6, 26, 28–30, 36–7, 49, 52, 54–5, 73, 82, 84, 87, 89, 90, 93–5, 97–100, 104, 158–9, 167, 170

New York City, 7, 9, 10, 14, 16–20, 22–3, 25–7, 30–1, 36–7, 41–3, 47, 49, 54, 58–60, 74, 83–4, 95–7, 100, 108, 112, 119, 123, 131, 133–7, 145, 152–4, 158, 160, 164, 167, 169–70

Ogden, Matthew, 22

Paris, 148, 152
Peekskill, 54
Pendleton, Nathaniel, 165, 167–9
Pennsylvania, 50–1, 54, 87, 128, 139, 161–2
Philadelphia, 9, 25, 28, 30, 36, 40, 43, 49–52, 55, 58–9, 62, 71, 81–2, 88–93, 106, 109, 113–5, 119–21, 128–31, 151–2, 164, 170
Pickering, Timothy, 151
Pinckney, Charles Cotesworth, 154
Pinckney, Thomas, 139–41, 154
Potomac River, 74, 109, 113, 116, 152
Poughkeepsie, 95–7, 103, 159
Princeton (College of New Jersey), 10, 22–3, 43
Putnam, Israel, 54–5

Randolph, Edmund, 118
Reynolds, James, 128–32, 142, 144
Reynolds, Maria, 129–32, 141–3, 146, 160
Rhode Island, 62
Richmond, 98
Rivington, James, 36
Rochambeau, Count de, 72–4, 76
Rodgers, John, 18

St. Clair, Arthur, 123–4
St. Croix, 3, 4, 6, 9–14
St. Kitts, 5
Saratoga, 52, 54, 59, 65

Schuyler, Philip, 64–6, 75–6, 78, 163
Schuylkill River, 50–1, 57
Scotland, 4, 158
Seabury, Samuel, 29–33
Smith, Melancton, 97–100
South Carolina, 47–8, 60–2, 139–40, 154, 157
Spain, 46
Staten Island, 22, 41
Steuben, Frederick von, 56–7
Stevens, Edward, 9, 10, 13

Talleyrand, Charles Maurice de, 148
Trenton, 43
Troup, Robert, 79, 131, 134

Valley Forge, 55–8, 69, 71
Van Ness, William P., 165, 167–9
Venable, Abraham, 128–30, 141, 143–4
Venton, Ann Lytton, 9, 10
Vermont, 156n, 157
Virginia, 24, 37, 50, 58, 69, 76, 87–8, 93–4, 96, 98, 110, 113, 118, 126, 128, 135, 141–2, 144–5, 155

Walker, Benjamin, 57
Washington, D.C., 113, 155, 170
Washington, George, 34, 40–3, 45–62, 65–6, 68–9, 72–7, 89, 92, 101–2, 109–10, 113–4, 117–8, 124, 127, 129, 135, 138–40, 150–2, 154, 161, 163
Washington, Martha, 62–3, 135
Wayne, Anthony, 48
Webster, Noah, 84–5
Weehawken, 160, 166, 171
Weeks, Levi, 134–5
Westchester, 29–30, 42
West Indies, 3–6, 9, 11, 14–5, 30, 69, 76, 85, 140n, 166
West Point, 72, 86
West Virginia, 142
Whitpain, 51–2
William and Mary College, 142
Williamsburg, 142
Witherspoon, John, 22–3
Wolcott, Oliver, 130

Yale University, 29
York, 51
Yorktown, 76–7, 151